Leading Mindfully

by

Pete Burden and Rob Warwick

Copyright

Copyright © 2015 Pete Burden and Rob Warwick

All rights reserved.

The authors have asserted their rights to be identified as authors of this work in accordance with the Copyrights, Designs, and Patents Act 1988.

No part of this publication may be reproduced, distributed, or transmitted in any form or by any means, including photocopying, recording, or other electronic or mechanical methods, without the prior written permission of the publisher, except in the case of brief quotations embodied in critical reviews and certain other non-commercial uses permitted by copyright law.

Published by Pete Burden and Rob Warwick.

For permission requests, please write to the publishers by email: info@seestep.com

ISBN-13: 978-1508870029 (paperback)

First edition.

10 9 8 7 6 5 4 3 2 1

Dedication

To Chog, Will and Joe.

To Linda, Ella and Jimmy.

Table of Contents

Preface

1 Introduction

2 It's a complex world

3 The stories we tell

4 The bumpy ride of noticing

5 Small changes

6 Power is real

7 To gossip and enquire

8 The mindful leader

9 Noticing, naming and holding

10 Practice – for the individual

11 Practice – in groups

12 Ending… and beginning

References

About the authors

Preface

'And never have I felt so deeply at one and the same time so detached from myself and so present in the world.' –
Albert Camus

How this book came about

Perhaps we came to this in a slightly different way from some who write about leading and leadership.

Back in 2012 we were both involved in starting a group called Conscious Business UK.

This was a group of people interested in different ways to do business. It was the time of Occupy with people protesting about the corrupting influence of business. Fed up with the obvious alternatives, over a period of about a year or so, some 500 people came together in different ways to ask questions, to try to find new ways forward.

These weren't people who wanted to denounce business. They were students, experienced business people, entrepreneurs, fleeing City bankers, and people from the digital economy to name a few.

One thing we immediately discovered is that there are many different understandings of the term 'Conscious Business'.

Yes, some people were interested in topics like CSR (Corporate Social Responsibility) and Social Enterprise. But most also wanted to get beyond those ideas. They wanted to find new ways to integrate the excitement, power and pleasure of business with positive outcomes for all humanity – but they weren't sure how.

They were also noticing that there were global problems that business was failing to solve: inequality, poverty, climate change, resource shortages, war etc.

They noticed that sometimes business, in their view, was making things worse, not better. Indeed, every day we hear stories of corporate misdeeds – aggressive tax avoidance, mis-selling of financial products, poor and unsafe working conditions (particularly for those with little or no voice), environmental harms, and so on.

They also, like us, noticed that businesses themselves were failing, perhaps unnecessarily. Did Blockbuster, Woolworths in the UK and countless others 'drift off', into a stupor of complacency? Did they fall asleep?

Was the same thing happening with public sector organisations and even society at large? Take health care, for example: the scandal of the Mid Staffordshire NHS Trust which led to hundreds losing their lives.

They also noticed that 'leaders' – those with positional power – were held up as saviours and heroes, and put on some kind of pedestal. A pedestal they did not always seem to deserve.

Unsure what to do about all this, these people came along to find fellowship, to enquire into these issues and to try to find a way forward.

It struck us that every one of them was leading.

Most of them thought business was a good thing. But they also thought the 'journey' was as important as the destination. Many saw money as 'fuel', fuel to drive personal growth and the impact the business has. Many realised they needed to change their own behaviour and attitudes, and the futility of trying to change others.

Many were open to, or practising, 'mindfulness', or something similar. Many spoke about becoming more 'aware', or more 'conscious'. Through our conversations practice and ideas were developing, and new awareness was emerging.

We'd been writing independently about these kinds of ideas for some years, and we decided there might be value in writing together. We started by asking a dozen people to write about their experience of 'Conscious Business'. Their stories can be found in two volumes of the AMED[1] journal e-Organisations and People (Warwick and Burden 2013, Burden and Warwick 2014).

If you're like these people, are curious and think there might be a better way to do business, then we wrote this book for you. We're simply exploring some of these ideas

---

[1] Association for Management Education and Development http://www.amed.org.uk/

further – especially the idea that becoming more aware as we do business is of great value.

Thanks and acknowledgements

We are not claiming to be masters of this ourselves, and everything we say here we have learnt from others. We're simply stumbling from one step to the next, and this writing is a record of a small part of that journey.

Major thanks must go to our long list of influences, some of whom you will find listed in the footnotes and references.

We also want to thank the many clients and colleagues we have worked with over the years for so graciously putting up with our stumbling, and helping us learn.

1 Introduction

In 140 characters or less:

'Appreciate that life, and work, is complex. Notice and enquire, especially how you relate to others.'

Many of us find business to be fun and rewarding. Doing something you care about and seeing an idea catch on is one of the greatest feelings in the world. It is also brilliant when you see people develop and grow – seeing, for example, someone who left school or university only recently confidently taking on new and more rewarding challenges.

All of this and at the same time you are making money for yourself and your family, and you're often adding something to your local community. Your business may also be making a much broader contribution: providing valuable goods and services, educating people, enhancing their health, or dealing with complex and important problems like climate change.

But business and working life isn't always like this.

Many people dread Monday mornings. There are stressful relationships and difficult breakups at work. Greed, unfairness, bullying, lies, cheating – these are all words that have come to be linked with business and working life.

Trust is destroyed, communities are affected, life savings are wiped out, and our environment is wrecked, as we continue to fail to solve the bigger problems of life: creating happiness and well-being, and dealing with global poverty, sickness, injustice, and war.

So what is going on?

Our experience is that nearly everyone we speak to wants to enjoy the former, more positive picture of work, not the latter. But somehow we find ourselves stuck in a repeating loop of 'business as usual'. It can be a negative spiral, and hard to escape from.

Thousands of books and articles and TED talks seem to suggest the solution is simple. That the world is easy to navigate, that it is clean cut, and clear what to do. That all you have to do is follow steps 'one, two and three' and everything will work out fine.

There is some great writing on a 'new' leadership out there – explaining how things work at a psychological (e.g. Rock 2009), behavioural (e.g. Kofman 2006), organisational (e.g. Laloux 2014) or systems level (e.g. Mackey and Sisodia 2014).

We're admirers, but at the same time we're cautious about 'explanations' and simple prescriptions. In our experience these tend to diminish rather than add to our ability to notice and engage in our own personal experience, reflection and practice.

We believe the day-to-day reality of being in business and in working life is very different from how it is commonly set out. In reality, it is messy, confusing, laden with difficult and unexplained emotion, full of false starts and missed stops.

It is never clear what is going on or why and all we seem able to do is just muddle along. Every now and then we think we have a solution, but like as not it will dissipate before our very eyes.

We may also have a sense that something is missing, that big parts of the story aren't being told. Or indeed that the story itself isn't something we can quite agree with?

Is business really as neat as popular TV programmes like 'Dragon's Den' and 'The Apprentice' suggest? Is there more going on beneath the veneer?

A way forward

So, if any of this rings true, rather than focusing on the theory, on the big picture, how about focusing on the mundane? The everyday.

For example, think of what you have done over the last few days at work. The chances are that you spent a lot of time in meetings, talking to people, making plans, trying to interpret what's happened, working out next steps.

You probably exchanged news and views and thoughts about other people. In other words, you had a bit of a gossip.

You may well have been confused, and faced with contradictory evidence or advice. The stakes might have been high, contracts to win or lose, and people's jobs (perhaps yours) at risk.

All this rolled up with emotions: anxiety, a fear of appearing foolish or out of your depth, anger, hope, concern, and sometimes just a 'buzz' – all rubbing along with your 'rational side'.

You know other people are influencing you. As you are probably influencing them. In ways you just cannot quite determine.

Muddling through

In short, it is complex and we should not delude ourselves that it is anything else.

Our premise in this book is that this should not paralyse us or cause us to seek sanctuary in promises of simplicity.

Instead, we believe we can work our way through things, perhaps not making the right decision every time (even trying might paralyse us), but making good enough decisions with what we have at hand.

To do this we need to notice, we need to enquire, we need to speak up about what is going on. We need to manage ourselves and our emotions, and somehow find a way to do this while in complex relationships with other people. We need to learn to help others do the same things. In short, we need to lead more mindfully.

Rivers of conversation

As we will explore, this is not as easy as it sounds. To do it we need to enter the conversation – like we enter a river.

Leading mindfully is often about changing the conversation. So we decided to write much of this book as a conversation, a dialogue, to give a sense of that flow.

In a conversation one person says something, another responds, and sometimes something new and unexpected emerges. There is no 'right', no end point – just an endless flow of ideas, a river of words and meaning.

We can't stop the river, but we can speed up, slow down, or change course. We can swim towards one bank or another, although we may not get there. We may bump into other people, then continue on our way.

And when we change what we say or how we say it we sometimes end up in unexpected places.

We believe being more conscious, more aware of our ability to change what we say, to change direction within the flow, is very important.

We believe there should be more of that in business, instead of the routine conversations that sometimes seem to dominate.

The dominant narrative

We also think there is a dominant narrative – a paradigm – about business, leadership and management. A way of understanding, thinking and talking that is broadly unhelpful to humanity. A way that affects how the water in the river generally flows.

Is business all about making money? Is it like war? It is like sport?

Paradigms can help, but they can also get in the way. They 'frame' the conversation and can seem to limit the options we have. What we see and what we do.

We're going to touch on some of these 'limitations' in this book, and hopefully test them.

Is the world simple, or complex? Can we control and predict what happens? Is power a thing? Should leadership be reserved only for those of a particular class? Is it fair to use intellect as the main arbiter of power? Is 'action' always essential? Are we only individuals, and do we work best individually, and in competition?

These are some of the ideas we would like to test and explore.

But to break out of a conventional paradigm is difficult. It may make some of the ideas here a little difficult to grasp, at least on first reading. So we need to swim slowly, to listen and sense carefully, to reflect, and take one stroke at a time.

We'll be very happy if this book provokes a few moments of puzzlement or even disagreement, alongside the occasional meeting of minds.

How to read this book

You are probably best off reading this book more like a novel than a text book, from beginning to end, coming back to subjects that pique your interest.

The layout is as follows:

- This chapter (Chapter 1) provides an introduction.
- Chapters 2, 3 and 4 introduce the theoretical underpinnings.
- Chapters 5, 6, 7, 8, and 9 expand on these and explore some practical examples.
- Chapter 10 and 11 outline some of practices we have found helpful for deepening awareness.
- Chapter 12 sums up and suggests a way forward.

We refer to books, articles and films and give some examples from our own lives. Some of these we explore in detail, others less so. Our aim is to provide a flavour of our own experiences and how we made sense of them.

Next steps

We hope you will follow up, test these ideas in the real world, and engage in conversations about the results with your colleagues and friends. These conversations are where we as individuals interact with the social melee in which we find ourselves.

Maybe it's the challenge we receive, and give, that makes sure we stay conscious and don't fall asleep?

And we *can* influence things. We believe we can change ourselves, and challenge those we work with through the conversations we have. Some may have more power than others, but no one is powerless, and we can all lead, and try to make things better.

Chapter summary

— There are many things not right with the world – businesses fail, and the human race faces many complex and intractable problems.

— Business, and the world of work, is a lot more complex than we might believe.

— There are different ways to lead. Everyone can lead. Leadership means noticing and enquiring, including with those around us.

— Paradigms and metaphors affect what we say and see. There's always power to consider. But we're not powerless, far from it.

— Life, and leading, is a conversation – dive into it.

2 It's a complex world

> *'Systems thinking is useful, but don't forget we are immersed; what we do makes a big difference to what happens around us.'*

Pete says: Sometimes, Rob, I am really struck by how complex it all is.

Like more and more people these days, I have my own business. I work hard, that is, I really put in the hours. In fact, I think about the business for nearly every waking minute.

I try to do the right thing with my colleagues. I want all of us to have a fulfilling life, and enjoy our work, as well as making enough money to meet our needs.

But it is really hard, at any point, to know what is the next best step. To try to balance all of the multiple needs and aims and choose what to do next.

I think I have learned over the years to look at the business systemically. I understand that one thing is connected to another, in ways that are hard to see and hard to predict. But that knowledge doesn't always seem to help.

Rob replies: I know, it can be horribly difficult to work out the next move. The question we often seem to be asking ourselves is *how to change things*. I am not sure it is the right question.

I think it is helpful to remember that historically a business was seen as a self-contained entity that was largely insulated from the external environment.

That assumption meant managers tried to exert direct control over staff, suppliers and even customers. It was a mechanical model of management – imagine a series of levers, pulleys and pistons between those in control and those to be controlled.

Pete: Yes, and there is a mind-set that the manager is in 'command' and has perfect information from which to make confident decisions. The manager is outside the business from where they can control it?

Rob: That's it.

Charlie Chaplin's film Modern Times (Chaplin, 1936) offers a vivid satirical commentary on this style of management and its implications[2]. It is easy to assume that the modern workplace is very different.

---

[2] The first few minutes of the film, available on YouTube makes the point vividly including: the production line speed being controlled by the boss with his burly staff pulling and pushing levers on his command, widespread surveillance including in washrooms and efforts to make the workforce more productive and less thoughtful. Of course, all this comes unstuck when Chaplin gets involved.
(https://www.youtube.com/watch?v=DfGs2Y5WJ14)

But when I use this film in my teaching and I ask the students (many of whom have part time jobs or are mature students with several years' work experience) to reflect on their own experience of work they readily relate to:

— The surveillance that they are subject to, particularly those who have worked in call centres, and the impact this has on their behaviour[3].

— The way work is broken down into component parts. This reduces the sense of being part of a social group, and the sense of creating something of value that people can identify with[4].

— The sense that work itself becomes little more than submitting to systems and bureaucracy[5].

This has a very real effect on them and the organisations they work for. It reduces the ability to collaborate. They

---

[3] Michel Foucault, the French philosopher and social theorist, explored the implications of surveillance by discussing Jeremy Bentham's Panopticon, a form of prison where the prison warder could see what the inmates were up to, but the prisoners were unaware when they were being watched. Over time, it was believed, the prisoner would self-regulate their behavior, on the assumption that they might be being watched, and this would lead to a longer term change compliant with the law.

[4] The concept of alienation was a main theme for Karl Marx. He explored this from a number of perspectives including the impoverishing effect it had on people's relationships with others, particularly as we are naturally sociable creatures; how the process of productive activity has a positive effect on the development of self and self-worth; and, the loss of control the employee experiences when they lose sight of the overall thing they are producing.

[5] This was an important theme that the sociologist Max Weber addressed over the course of his career.

don't engage. They come to work and switch off. They do what they are told but they don't use their brains, creativity, enthusiasm or sense of fun.

Pete: That's a great example. That seems to be exactly the kind of thing that many people coming to Conscious Business meetings are reacting to. They hate the sense of being controlled, and being a part in a machine. Everywhere I see people calling out for empowerment, and flexibility, and to be allowed to 'be themselves'.

More and more of these people go off and start their own businesses or social enterprises. Starting a business is seen as the ultimate form of self-expression in 2015.

But many of them also seem to want to be in control themselves!

Before long, if the business survives at all, I hear the MDs of start-ups and SMEs complaining about their teams and colleagues, and how they won't do what they are asked, or told.

Rob: I think that despite the appearance of control in businesses – in the form of procedures, policies, boards, requirements of confidentiality, processes of inclusion and exclusion etc – it sometimes helps to ask "Who is really in control?". Where does power lie, both within and beyond the organisation?

Despite what people might say and what is written down it is hard to find who actually has ultimate power. Doing nearly everything requires collaboration and consent.

Perhaps a better way to think about it is that we are all caught up in a web of power relations, each affecting each other in different ways. I think it is helpful to notice this more.

Pete: Yes. When we discuss these things at Conscious Business meetings people often say, with a laugh, that they don't do what they are asked to do anyway. People seem to show great creativity in ignoring or getting around directives from 'above'.

And that is certainly my experience. Even when I have nominally been in charge, been the 'leader', it really doesn't feel that way, or work out that way. I certainly can't lead by standing at the front waving a flag. That doesn't work for me.

Rob: I think leadership and 'followership' are probably unhelpful ideas, when simplified too much. I think it is better to consider leadership and followership as behaviours – not as roles. And as complementary and connected behaviours that we all adopt from time to time.

So instead we might see leading (or following) as sitting in a network of interdependent relationships. We are in a system that is developing over time as the people in it influence and are influenced by each other's power. Relationships are built up over many years. This affects how we get on, and what we achieve.

Pete: The problem is that often these relationships go unnoticed – especially to those who are inside the network, inside the organisation, and used to it.

Rob: And from the outside it all seems quite crazy – what is happening is often quite unfathomable to those who are new to the situation[6].

Pete: I also understand the dangers of thinking about the business as a machine. If I adopt that point of view, I can easily fall into the trap of believing that by pulling the right levers things might change or get better.

I can also imagine that I am 'adding a catalyst' or 'cleaning out the arteries'. Or 'adding fertiliser' to the system. But I also know that all these are models. Mechanical, chemical, bodily or ecosystem models.

And whatever model I use it may lead me to focus on 'cause and effect' – to believe that if I do something to the system, something else will happen.

This is the danger of all models – they are useful to help us understand and communicate ideas. But, if they become fixed, then they can get in the way of perception.

Rob: Using a model also brings with it the perhaps unrealistic idea of an ideal state where the system will naturally come to some sort of equilibrium if only the right 'formula' is found.

I think using the idea of systems as a way of understanding an organisation, an economy, or a sector

---

[6] The French sociologist and anthropologist Pierre Bourdieu noted 'when you read, in Saint-Simon, about the quarrel of hats (who should bow first), if you were not born in a court society, if you do not possess the habitus of a person of the court, if the structures of the game are not also in your mind, the quarrel will seem futile and ridiculous to you. If, on the other hand, your mind is structured according to the structures of the world in which you play, everything will seem obvious and the question of knowing if the game 'is worth the candle' will not even be asked' (Bourdieu 1998).

can be helpful. It is a way of thinking that puts attention on the non-linear and complex dynamics that can play out.

Usually when people talk about systems in relation to business they mean it is worthwhile to consider the parts (or 'nodes'), the interactions between those parts, the whole system and what lies outside.

One consequence is that a single initial interaction can lead to unpredictable consequences. Together the multitude of interconnections mean the system as a whole is extremely difficult to predict, and impossible to control.

Pete: Yes, it's the illusion of control that often gets in my way.

Rob: I think it is also important to realise, and to accept, that none of us lives beyond the 'system'. We are all immersed in the system and, as we affect others, so others come to affect us.

Pete: I frequently hear people calling the leaders 'them' or 'they'. The people at the 'top'[7] (Oshry 1999) also talk about their teams as 'they'. Both seem to think that the business or organisation is doing something *to* them, and that it needs to be brought under control.

This is very different from the sense of really being part of something, where I am an equal and important part of the system.

---

[7] Barry Oshry's (Oshry 1999) work on groups supports the idea that people naturally fall into these roles: top, middle, and bottom, and then experience the organisational consequences of each role.

I think we're all 'co-creating' the system. We all contribute to the results we get.

Of course, I have to acknowledge I can see myself forgetting that I am one of the participants too. I'll give you an example.

Some years ago I was working on a venture with some colleagues when a new person joined.

It was still early days and so, when he suggested 'stopping' completely while we re-thought things, I thought it was a great idea. I believe such projects need to 'pivot' often if they are to find their own direction.

'Stopping' meant taking my foot of the accelerator. As soon as I did – as soon as I stopped making myself go to meetings and explaining the project, for example – I noticed something in myself. I noticed how much I was 'pushing' things.

At first, I wondered where this desire to push things was coming from? My previous experience? My assumptions about the best way to run things? Even my childhood experience – had I always been someone who pushed?

Stopping also made me realise something important about the group dynamic. Here I was pushing, pushing, going to meetings, driving for change. I noticed I felt resentful that the others didn't seem to be pushing as hard as me.

Our internal meetings usually started and ended with me trying to push something through. I introduced new ideas that I thought were really essential. But everything I introduced seemed to cause a problem with my colleagues. Eventually I realised this was 'resistance' – a response to my pushing.

'Stopping' made me aware that I was at least partially responsible for what was happening in our group. As I stopped pushing, the resistance also seemed to disappear. In other words, I was creating the resistance.

I can't quite remember how it came about, but one day one of my colleagues told me he was content with the way the project was going. This was a huge shock to me – because I certainly wasn't content – with the rate of growth, the financial success etc.

I hadn't noticed this difference between us. I think the pushing – and the resultant resisting – had stopped me from seeing what was really going on. From noticing what was really happening, in the present. I didn't realise that my colleagues and I had quite different views of reality.

Not that any of us was right. But it was very surprising to discover that we had different views and quite possibly different aims. While we were locked in 'pushing' and 'resisting the pushing' it somehow seemed very difficult to find that out.

All this really helped me realise that I am part of the system. I am not distinct from it, pushing it along from outside, or controlling it. I am a really important and equal part of what is happening.

Chapter summary

— The world is 'complex'. It is very hard to predict and impossible to control.

— It isn't a physical 'system', one that we are outside and can control.

— We're in it, and part of it, and how we see it, and what we do as a result, affects what happens.

— Leading and following are behaviours, and one is connected to the other in a dynamic way.

— Pushing or trying to control can get in the way of seeing what is happening – really being aware and mindful.

3 The stories we tell

'The power of stories lies in building bridges of shared understanding. But if only it was that easy!'

Rob says: I think social systems, and our own unique understanding from being immersed in them, gradually unfold as we all inch forward together. We are stuck in patterns that are, at the same time, both surprising and new and reassuringly similar. We recognise our habits, and the things we do over and over again. But we also recognise those moments of newness – when something different or unexpected happens.

Through the lens of history, we can see there are multiple viewpoints, multiple actors, and no one is in control.

For example, consider the Black Power movement in 1960s America. From our vantage point today we might see a body of force and resistance, some of which was organised, some disorganised.

But we can also imagine a growing communal sense of injustice building up over generations. Then there are some seminal moments, defiant steps – such as those of Rosa Parks who sat on a seat in a bus reserved for white people – that created a spark that drew worldwide attention to the cause and built further determination for change.

This in turn led to further action – and inaction. And we are still feeling the ripples today. But at the same time it seems as if nothing has changed. There is still much racial (and other) injustice in our world.

All of this gives a sense of how social movements are paradoxical and defy mechanistic control. No one is in absolute 'control', whatever might be claimed after the fact.

Pete replies: Of course, there have also been big changes in the broader context. The arrival of social media really has changed things: the numbers of conversations we have, their speed, how we shape what influences us, and how we shape the conversation with others.

Rob: Yes, in system terms, there are many more nodes and interactions.

There is no 'one story'. There are many, as many as the people who choose to give the matter thought and to articulate their experience.

It is in forming and sharing these differing stories that we move to a shared narrative. Bearing in mind that there is never a complete overlap of meaning. Meaning is continually forming and different for everyone involved.

Some stories become cultural reference points, like beacons from which we can navigate and make sense of our interactions with others. Others fade.

These beacons incite and invite further response, and further shared meaning making.

Take Rosa Parks' story again. For some, it was a carefully planned premeditated act. For others, there was a degree of opportunism. For many, it doesn't matter which it was – compared with the backdrop of social injustice stretching back generations.

People's views are shaped by their history. And people's views of history affect their future. Both have further bearing on their story. A white supremacist and an activist in the black power movement will have some shared understanding of what happened, but also a lot of disagreement.

Pete: Yes, I see that. I am telling you a story about that project. I know it is only a story. As I said I can't quite remember the details. My experience of this is that the story becomes firmer and clearer the more I tell it. But I also know that my story may be diverging from reality as I tell and re-tell it.

I also know that my colleagues would tell very different stories. They probably saw it all quite differently from me.

This is something we all do, all the time. We make up 'stories' to fit what appears to us to be the 'facts'. The problem is that the stories also affect what we think we see – we select facts to support the story.

Another way to understand this is that 'meaning is found in the response' (Mead 1934). How you respond to what I say determines the meaning of what I say. For example, a shout can be heralding an aggressive act. Or it might be a warning. It all depends on how the hearer interprets it.

Rob: Yes, there is little absolute meaning in human conversation – only what we believe to be true.

Pete: And, of course, we're all coming at things from different points of view. That means all these different perspectives get mixed up. In that sense we are all contributing equally to the results we get.

However much it is tempting to blame others, or blame ourselves, the results are really emerging from the way we work together, the way we see the world, and what we feel about it.

Rob: Meaning seems to emerge and develop all the time. At least, that is my sense of it.

I am also part of that emerging story. I exist in relation to how others see me – I am a reflection of what others think of me.

Pete: Yes, and that is all a bit scary, but it seems truer to me than a more fixed view of reality[8].

I don't see how we can stop making sense in this way.

Metaphors and stories, of course, are important in how we communicate. But they also limit our thinking, our thinking affects what we do[9].

---

[8] See the work of Kenneth Gergen, known for the comment 'I am linked therefore I am' – stressing a relational view of human existence (Gergen 2009).

[9] The work of George Lakoff suggests that the metaphors we use to explain complexity significantly affect our lives. See e.g. "Metaphors we live by" (Lakoff and Johnson 2003).

So it is helpful to be aware of the metaphors we use, such as 'business is war'.

Rob: The other thing that I think often happens when we put ourselves outside of the system is that the so-called 'leaders' – by which I mean the people with positional power, the people at the 'top' – spend their time trying to develop 'strategies' to control the system.

These strategies rely on 'perfect' information to predict what will happen if we do one thing or another.

Afterwards, when the strategy has been 'executed' (that, in itself, is a very particular kind of language!) a story is constructed which proves the strategy to have been the right one.

I think this is fraught with danger and disappointment[10]; particularly if it is at the expense of developing a conscious awareness of the dynamics of the 'now'.

Pete: Yes. 'History is written by the victors'[11]. But I think it is helpful to remember that we are all doing this, all the

---

[10] The writings of the systems thinker and operational researcher, Stafford Beer, are telling. In his collection of essays Think Before You Think: Social Complexity and Knowledge of Knowing, edited by David Whittaker, he describes his work with the Chilean president Salvador Allende in the 1970s. Under Beer's guidance computers were installed to predict and control the Chilean economy. It was visionary cybernetics where circular causal relationships were there to be identified and controlled leading to prosperity and social justice for all. What could not be controlled were external economic and political factors. There was a coup, facilitated by its powerful neighbour to the North. Allende died. Stafford Beer was deeply affected by the events and failure of the system (Beer 2009).

[11] Quote often attributed to Winston Churchill.

time. It isn't just the victors who write a story. So does everyone else, including the losers.

Rob: And I think there is a way to lead in business that is about being aware of the patterns of relationships we are part of, and then acting upon them. Being aware of the patchwork of overlapping themes from which we all continue to develop meaning.

It means not only developing our own consciousness but also enabling others to do the same in the conversations we have with them. In this way, consciousness moves from the individual to the social. I think this is a better way to understand leadership: as about developing collective consciousness. On the one hand, it is meaningful to the group. And, on the other, it is also meaningful to the individual.

Pete: What about the risk we mentioned earlier? That working as part of a team, in a department, or within an organisation, ways of acting, behaving and thinking become so normalised that we don't notice them at all? We stop discussing them with others.

Rob: Lots of what goes on in a department might well be efficient and purposeful. But lots also might also be wasteful or damaging. Who notices? When a new member of staff turns up and asks "Why is this happening …?" suddenly there is an opportunity to notice.

But social cohesion and conformity are very powerful, and this noticing and talking about it starts to diminish quickly, even in just a few days.

Pete: Have you ever seen those great Candid Camera videos (Beck 2014)? The man in the lift? With the hat? And then there is the work of Solomon Asch[12]? These show the power of group conformity very starkly.

It is hard to accept how much of what we do is driven by the behaviour of the groups we are in. We are so often told we are individuals in control of our own lives.

Rob: And of course we *are* in control as individuals too – when we make conscious choices about how we act. I think the more conscious leader seeks to develop awareness of what they can control, and tries to let go of what they cannot.

Pete: I can see that. I can work on my own awareness – inner and outer. By investing the time to sense what is going on and to learn and understand more.

This means noticing what is happening in others, in the group, and in myself. Within myself, I can notice my current thoughts, but also my feelings and emotions. Sensations from my body as I move and, of course, my five senses.

Then there are my hopes, my dreams and my aspirations, my memories about the past, my intuitions, my instincts and probably more.

---

[12] Social psychologist Solomon Asch's experiments showed the power of group conformity – many subjects when in a situation where others seemed to be seeing something different, would change what they reported to fit the apparent norm. See e.g. https://vimeo.com/61349466 (Conformity – Elevator Candid Camera) and http://www.youtube.com/watch?v=qA-gbpt7Ts8 (The Solomon Asch Conformity Experiment).

That is quite a big job in itself.

Rob: Yes, it is. And, as I said, leadership is about helping others develop that noticing ability too.

That can be quite risky. People don't always like having their usual patterns of how they relate to each other changed. So drawing attention to this needs to be carefully considered and negotiated in the moment.

But there are lots of ways to do this. As I become more conscious of my own behaviour, I might choose to change it. For example, I might present a board paper in a different way – in a visual format, or in summary form.

I might ask people who would not normally work together to collaborate. I might encourage people to take on different roles, I might choose an unfamiliar location for a meeting, or just arrange the meeting room differently. All of these might encourage people to notice things differently and encourage alternative patterns of conversations.

And then I can also make an overt invitation to the group to notice and reflect on how things are and what they are noticing.

Pete: One thing I sometimes do in meetings is to invite people to notice what is happening in the group. A simple example is to start a meeting by asking people to say how they are feeling.

Not what they think, but how they feel[13]. Sometimes someone will reveal something that was previously

---

[13] It is a curiosity of our language that the phrase 'I feel that' or 'I feel like' usually does not refer to feelings at all. It means what I think, or how I interpret what is going on. Feelings are, of

unknown – perhaps they will say they are feeling a bit anxious, for example.

Another approach is simply to encourage an open and enquiring mind-set. This can be done by inviting people to to discuss what the future might look like. Or to step back from the process we are in, and wonder more broadly about the next steps involved in making something happen.

Sometimes I ask people what **questions** they are bringing. This is so different from expecting people to come to meetings with **answers**.

This approach starts with 'not knowing', more than knowing the answer. That's what I call 'enquiry'.

Rob: Another idea is to encourage the group to discuss and notice uncertainty within the system. To point out that it is all more complex[14] than we would sometimes like to see it.

A good way to do this is to ask people to offer their different perspectives on what is happening. And to tolerate that difference – this reveals how dependent meaning is on perspective and context.

Pete: Or we may highlight values, and ask whether or not behaviour is aligned with these.

---

course, more visceral, in the body. 'I feel anxious' is a description (using words) of a sensation in the body.

[14] See the work of Ralph Stacey, Doug Griffin and Patricia Shaw around the theory of organisations as complex responsive processes of relating (Griffin et al. 1998).

What different views do we have about transparency, about how decisions should be made, and by whom? How are people valued for what they do, how much should they get paid, and be rewarded?

Even though they are clearly important, many of these things are often not discussed openly, at least not with those they most affect.

There are always lots of differences of opinion, when we take the trouble to look. The trick is to tolerate – at least temporarily – these differences.

Rob: I agree. That is more how I understand leadership. It is about my noticing, and the way I go about things – helping people notice more of what is happening, and also what is not.

It may be difficult for the person who is 'leading' to admit that they don't know, or that things are complex and not simple.

Mostly I know I need to do that for myself. I need to calm myself and look more carefully at what is going on inside and outside of me. But it is inspiring to think of being able to help and support others by helping them notice more too.

Chapter summary

— There's no single story, no 'right' story. Meaning changes all the time. It depends on your point of view, and assumptions.

— Social media accelerates this – highlighting different and multiple points of view.

— We can easily fall asleep at the wheel – we can stop noticing, and instead succumb to group pressure.

— 'Leading' means drawing attention to all that. For ourselves and for others.

— As we do that, we'll start to notice differences in the ways people see the world. If we haven't fallen asleep!

4 The bumpy ride of noticing

'There's lots to notice; it can be difficult; we may need a jolt; not noticing has advantages, and risks too.'

Rob says: Much of the reason for coming together to write this book is that both of us believe that how we respond in a complex world is dependent upon what we are conscious of, and how we are conscious.

It might sound obvious – surely we are conscious all the time? But I don't think it is as straightforward as it seems. Largely because our routines – the habits we fall into with others – reduce our ability to see what is happening. We stop noticing, and in that sense our consciousness diminishes.

Perhaps we can talk first about noticing, and then about how we respond. That makes it sound as if the two are unconnected but I think they are highly 'enmeshed' – like a horse and carriage.

Pete replies: That's right. But shall we start with noticing? With being more mindful?

Rob: For me, noticing is the ability to see, feel and hear what is happening around us. In other words, to use our senses to the fullest extent and to couple this with our thoughts, memories and ways of understanding. Noticing is being aware of what is around us **and** how it might affect us. The two are totally bound together.

As we do this, we can also notice, and try to understand our own assumptions, biases, routines and habits. We become more 'mindful' of them. And perhaps we realise how that noticing and understanding gives us choices?

Sometimes an experience will jolt us in a startling way. Let me give an example.

Last week I popped into the pub and…

> *Not much time, a quick pint in The Ship. I sat down in a comfy tatty red chair. 'I can't cope' came a woman's voice over a wooden partition. 'I need to get home', loud, panicky, panting. The couple next to me stand up and peer over the partition – I sit. I notice my increased awareness, a 'meta-view' of the room, the people and me. Courtney, the pot-man, turns his head and says loudly 'I've got my own problems', turns back. I still have not seen this person but the people she is with stand up, shuffle around 'do you need an ambulance?' 'No … umm!' The pub is becoming quieter, my thoughts louder. She is sobbing now, gathering more attention. Help arrives …*[15]

The pub was as it had always been but the distress of this person and subsequent help that she received meant I noticed my usually routine experience in a different way.

---

[15] As we will see in Chapter 10, writing short narratives such as this can be helpful.

Pete: Yes, I understand. It reminds me of the film 'Groundhog Day', everything seems to repeat, but then I suddenly notice what is happening. It is as if I suddenly wake up, jolted out of my routine.

Anthony De Mello wrote very humorously about this in his book 'Awareness' (De Mello 1990).

There's lots to notice, isn't there? It isn't just noticing of ourselves as individuals, there are other layers too. For example:

— *The group, or team*. The people that we work with day in and day out. How do they go about things? How do people relate to each other? Who has power and how is it exercised, or not? What is seen as normal or strange?

— *The organisation*. A bigger group, everything is on a larger scale. What are the power dynamics between different teams and groups? What are the routines by which a person gets access, or not, to more senior colleagues or teams? What are the other means of inclusion and exclusion, and how do these affect what conversations can and can't happen?

— *The sector or industry or professional grouping*. How do all the organisations involved, and all the stakeholders, behave together? What are the norms and what is seen as 'good practice'? What does this enable and constrain in terms of new practices, innovation and what is seen as acceptable? How does this sector come to interact with others and where is the friction?

Rob: It can be overwhelming. But maybe we don't need to wait for traumatic events to wake us out of our dream. We can be proactive and go out of our way to notice.

Starting with the individual, there is a wealth of literature and advice on noticing. I really liked Iain McGilchrist's book 'The Master and his Emissary' (McGilchrist 2009). It is a new take on the divided brain – and about the paradoxical interaction between the left and right hemispheres of the brain.

Essentially, he argues that the left, logical brain has gained prominence in our society, diminishing our ability to notice the bigger picture.

Pete: Yes, it is a great example of how modern neuroscience is helping us understand ourselves in new ways. I love the work of Dan Siegel on what he calls 'Mindsight'[16] (Siegel 2010). Reminding us that the brain/body is very plastic and that we can continue to develop it well into later life, he also gives practical tools and advice on how to notice and become more conscious of all aspects of ourselves.

All the senses, the body, and the mind and emotions. He also suggests that we need to notice our relationships too – for him and others we are relational beings, embedded in a network of relationships with others.

Of course, this isn't just about sitting there contemplating our navels.

For example, we often talk about organisational behaviour as if it is a rational process of cool-headed decision-

---

[16] See http://www.drdansiegel.com/about/mindsight/

making. But think about it. Pay attention to – be mindful of – the point at which you need to make a difficult decision and how you go about this.

What might you notice? The emotion? Perhaps you are feeling a sense of anxiety, anticipation, hope, or even dread? How is this affecting your more rational process? Rather than dismissing these feelings as irrational, and giving primacy to the rational, maybe it is better to be aware of these feelings and how they are coming to affect our thinking, actions and interactions with others?

As we start to do that, we might also wonder where these emotions are coming from? Are they deep-seated and internal? Or are they related to the way we are reacting to something or someone around us? Or perhaps an interaction between the two?

Rob: There really is a lot going on here. Internally, and in our relationships. It strikes me how little of this we really discuss – especially in business and organisational settings. As if it is in some way not valid.

In business we often don't discuss emotion. And personally we may decide to suppress it, if it seems too difficult to raise.

Pete: Can we talk again about the stories we tell each other? Stories we tell about ourselves, our teams, organisations and the wider systems of which we are part. About the competition, customers or anyone who is not in our group.

What do these stories, and the language we use, tell us about the organisational culture that surrounds us, and that we are a part of?

Rob: Recently, for example, I facilitated a workshop with a group of doctors and senior clinical managers. People told stories about things like 'service redesign' and how 'clinical care pathways' had been developed in association with 'key stakeholders'. There was a lot of talk about the efficiencies gained and 'quality of outcomes'.

Suddenly one of the doctors told us she had noticed that we hadn't spoken about the patient other than in very abstract terms. This caused a moment of collective embarrassment.

The doctor not only noticed this, but she also gave us the opportunity to re-visit what was seen of as value by the group. The conversation on 'quality', 'stakeholders' and 'redesign' had many assumptions, not least that the whole system was something of a machine, and that it – the 'project' – was all about increasing efficiency.

By deciding to make her noticing public, she created a moment of collective noticing. We all felt a bit embarrassed, and we were also able to notice some of our assumptions.

Pete: Yes, it is the same in business, I think. When we speak of 'customers' what are the stories that we tell? Do we talk about how we win, and other people lose? Or is the story about creating value for everyone?

What are the fundamental assumptions we are making about our purpose, the purpose of business, the purpose of our organisations, and so on? How might this be affecting what we end up doing?

What stories are we making up about our colleagues? What do we think they are up to?

The Ladder of Inference[17] demonstrates how assumptions affect us in practical ways. It shows how we may make up stories about other people, and often fail to check them out. Two or more people may have completely different stories about a third.

Rob: And this is not just a cognitive, rational process. Our emotions and feelings significantly affect *what* we sense – what we see, hear etc. They also affect how mindful we are able to be – whether we are able to notice *how* we are thinking, and feeling.

Whether we are able to make our noticing public is also an issue. We may notice something but be too scared to point it out.

We all have many filters and biases, and a good way to start to notice these is to work with people who are different – for example, in thinking, age, attitude, race, gender etc.

Unconscious metaphors[18] are an example of how *the way* we think affects *what* we think. For example, in the meeting I mentioned above, there seemed to be a very mechanistic metaphor – about pathways and 'redesign'. When the doctor noticed we had been leaving out the

---

[17] Chris Argyris' Ladder of Inference. See e.g. Mindtools (2015).

[18] Gareth Morgan's (Morgan 2006) seminal study that describes the different ways that we frame 'organisations'.

patient, she was tending towards the nurturing and organic.

Perhaps we might all agree that nurturing and organic is more socially acceptable than the machine metaphor. But it is still a metaphor.

There are many other metaphors – such as war and battles, sport, the epic saga, brains, chemistry, telecommunication networks, and even metaphors for emergence. Even describing complexity in the way we are, as a river of conversation, is a metaphor. I hope it is helpful, but it is only what we are constructing in our minds.

I think it is worth noticing how these metaphors comfort us and help us form meaning. That kind of noticing gives us a little more choice. If we notice the metaphor, perhaps we can move beyond it?

Pete: I think we can. But first we have to be conscious, to notice.

Take another example. Consider your working environment, your office, where you have meetings, the furniture and so on. Even the reception area where visitors arrive is full of symbolic meaning.

What is this environment telling you about the culture of the organisation you work in and the way that you work with others?

One way to shake it all up is to change what we do. For example, on a project at BBC News back in 1997, largely by accident, we started having 'stand-up meetings'[19]. No chairs, no tables. Just people standing in a circle. They were shorter and snappier than most other meetings I have been in, before or since. The nature of the interaction was different, perhaps more intense.

This is all worth noticing. This is all about the context. A lot of work on communication focuses on what people say to each other. But I am trying to draw attention to the **context.** This includes the way the content of the conversation is 'framed' by the context, including the emotional context – how we feel.

Chapter summary

— Sometimes we need a jolt, to get us noticing.

— There's so much to notice. Our thoughts, feelings, moods. Our colleagues. The interactions between us all. It can be overwhelming.

— Language and metaphor tell us a lot. The 'system' is just a metaphor. Don't confuse the map with the territory (Korzybski 1931).

— Look out for assumptions – they can trip us up.

— Give a thought to the (emotional) context – and our filters and biases – as well as the content.

---

[19] This is not as unusual as it might seem. The Privy Council in the UK has held its meetings standing up since at least the reign of Queen Victoria, who apparently noticed it helped them finish sooner.

5 Small changes

'Sometimes it can be easier not to notice, but to notice is the first step in making a change.'

Rob says: When someone is new to an organisation they tend to see things clearly. They may be more conscious of what is happening. Sometimes this is laced with confusion and just trying to understand what is going on.

What is it that they find odd, peculiar or just funny? What is surprising and how?

These conversations have to be handled carefully as the person is still acclimatising, feeling vulnerable and cautious about making a good impression. Nevertheless, they are vital sources of insight.

Pete replies: Sometimes, when I visit clients or other organisations, I ask myself what surprises me and why. I mean, what I *see*, rather than just what they say. That can tell me a lot about the client.

But it is also a 'rear-view mirror' on my own organisation – the differences can tell me a lot about our own practice.

Rob: When you are busy working on a project it can be tempting to look inward, heads down, to get the work done and focus on the monthly performance figures. But, in lifting your head perhaps you might wonder who would be the champion or enthusiast for your work? Perhaps you can try to imagine what it is that they would be saying? Who would be the advocates and detractors and their reasons why?

Who is not in the room who might be affected?

This is an example of using your imagination to extend the way you notice. It is a way of exploring the context, not just the content. As we do this we are subtly creating new possibilities, new choices. For example, we might decide to go and have a conversation with one of those people.

Pete: Yes, this is a good way to introduce more choice.

There may also be things that are much harder to notice. From psychology, for example, comes the idea of 'transference'. In simple terms, this is when someone reminds us of another person – perhaps a parent. When we meet that person, our behaviour alters to reflect the relationship we had with the original person – even though they are not the same person at all.

This is just one example of the kind of processes that are going on all the time between people, in pairs and in groups. From this, we start to get the idea of a group 'dynamic' or 'matrix' – how people interact and interrelate, and what emerges from that interaction[20]. Obviously this can get very complex. And we often start out unconscious of it.

---

[20] Foulkes (1983) was one of the people who developed the idea of the group matrix. Authors like Farhad Dalal (Dalal 1998) urge us to take group phenomena seriously.

The thing to remember is that we are all responsible jointly for the results we get in the groups we are in. In many ways, the group has a life of its own – over and above what the individuals may think is happening. It is very easy to forget this.

Rob: I think there are also occasions and situations where *not* noticing may be useful.

If we are just interested in doing the same thing over and over again, as efficiently as possible, it may be better to do it in a way that favours 'un-thinking', and a lack of challenge towards any habits. Asking awkward questions and noticing may be seen as a distraction – perhaps it is stopping the organisation do what it does best?

Noticing and challenging come at a cost – both organisationally and personally. It therefore needs to be handled sensitively and carefully. It is a practice of itself. And, like any practice, it takes time to develop, and is richly dependent on the context. Is it welcomed or hated? And if so why?

Pete: It can create quite a lot of anxiety, can't it? If we start to look and enquire into what is really happening, we may discover things we are not quite sure we want to see.

But problems can also arise if we avoid noticing. Kodak, at the time a world leader in photography, apparently held many of the intellectual property rights for digital imaging. But perhaps it was blind to the opportunity, blinded by ways of doing things that had for so long held the company in good stead?

Did people in the company lose focus, or perhaps they weren't aware of their biases and assumptions?

Did this lack of mindfulness affect strategy? Did it affect how the company invested? Which products it brought to market?

It's an old example, but it does make me wonder. How many companies are head down and miss what is happening around them?

Rob: Yes, and the general assumption in many organisations seems to be that only people at the top are even allowed to have their heads up, to think strategically. I think this is an assumption well worth questioning.

Pete: As we have said, responding by noticing and by enquiring can be helpful. We can never know for sure, but we can at least imagine a different course of events when people respond in that way.

This is one way that noticing and responding are so connected. How we respond to a situation leads us to see the world differently. In seeing the world differently, we then may respond differently. And so it goes on.

Rob: I think even small changes in behaviour can lead to new ways of noticing, and therefore perhaps to different results.

For example, a chief executive in healthcare in the UK changed the way that board papers were to be written. She asked for them to be shorter, and immediately under the title they were to be summarised in 140 characters or less – a tweet.

This led to rumblings and discontent among executives who had been promoted for, among other things, their ability to carefully craft a long, well-reasoned paper.

For others it led to a ripple of excited talk. What was really valuable? What did it mean about the culture of the organisation, and could it be changed?

Pete: I like that example.

Of course, we need to be careful when we make these kinds of moves. If I have a particular course of action and destination in mind, some sort of argument or idea that I have already decided is best, then I am 'advocating'. I am holding a position and trying to persuade others to adopt it too.

The problem with advocacy is that it may generate resistance. Few of us like being told what to do. We may not show that – we may acquiesce but rebel in secret. Some people may go along – they may collude. When, actually, a dialogue of opposing points of view may be more useful.

In all these cases, power is at play. The group dynamic is at work. This is something to be aware of.

Rob: What's the alternative?

Pete: As I mentioned before, we can offer an 'enquiry'. In this case, the invitation is different. The assumption – the framing – is that no one is in control of what happens, and that everyone has a voice – a voice that itself can be noticed.

An advocacy such as "I think that board papers...." may close the conversation down. Whereas a genuine enquiry such as "Why do we write board papers in this particular way?" may open a conversation. We need to be careful not to hide an advocacy (for example, a criticism) behind a question. But, if it is based on real openness, enquiry may move things forward.

This is a really important part of modelling by the individual. By genuine enquiry, I mean, genuinely, authentically, and honestly approaching the situation with a sense of not knowing.

This is a way of being. It is not just a simple technique of language or a matter of learning to ask a particular type of question. It means addressing the world with real curiosity and wonder.

If the individual can adopt that position, and maintain it even for a short while, interesting things sometimes start to happen.

Rob: What we have been describing here is the role of the individual and their ability to affect the dynamics of the relationships of which they are part. To notice, to make changes, and to offer further reflection as to what this might mean.

These are very small 'gestures'. We may only be talking about a few words, quietly spoken. Of course, everybody – whatever their position – does and can make these kinds of gestures all the time. This is a major part of what is happening in an organisation – lots and lots of conversations following certain conversational rules or habits.

Can you imagine the effect of all of these thousands or even millions of conversational gestures? What do they mean for the wider system? What patterns emerge? We can see patterns in policies, in culture, in how people in the organisation describe their organisation, in the stories, and in the themes that are used.

I think it is important not to underestimate the impact of changes to these gestures – whether by noticing or through the response. Even small changes may be noticed and picked up by others very quickly. They may spread virally.

Take a simple change like the 140-character board paper summary. This may start to affect how group discussions are held more widely. Maybe other people will start to summarise?

Set against this are those vested interests that seek to keep things just as they are.

Pete: But this is a dynamic where no one is in absolute control, even if some have more influence than others.

An idea may take off. Or it may not. No one can control that, but we can notice what happens.

And, when an idea takes off, it is likely that there will be some after-the-fact sense-making by the powerful groups – the directors, senior management etc. They will take ownership and explain that it was all part of a 'plan'.

This, in itself, maintains the narrative of control – through the idea that there was a plan, and it was neatly executed.

Rob: Yes, the stories go round and round.

Chapter summary

— Are you new to the conversation? Don't miss that opportunity.

— There is always an underlying dynamic. Ignore it at your peril.

— Sometimes it may be beneficial not to notice.

— If we notice things, we can start to make small changes. Is it better to advocate a change, or to enquire into it?

— None of this means we can predict or control what will happen. But we can keep noticing.

6 Power is real

'Power is everywhere. Noticing's the antidote. Stay in the conversation, and keep an eye out for what becomes unnoticed.'

Pete says: So, what we're saying is, 'it seems complex, because it is'. That sense that I sometimes have that the world is complex and difficult to understand doesn't mean there is something wrong with me! Actually, the world *is* complex and difficult to understand, and it is very sane to experience it that way?

Rob replies: Yes, I think so. That's certainly how I experience it too. Noticing helps. And, as we mentioned in the previous chapter, one of the most important things we can notice is group dynamics. We are often unconscious of these. They seem to operate just underneath the surface, and one of the most important dynamics is 'power'.

Pete: That's a really weighty word Rob, 'power'. Sometimes I think if I could get power, and the relationships that go with it, 'right' then everything would work out better.

But that is hard. Running a small business, I often don't seem to have enough power to get things done. Other people, and bigger organisations, often seem to have the upper hand – they just seem to have more power than me.

Rob: Yes. One way to understand power is that it is a major force by which things are achieved, destroyed, subverted or won. That other people have more power than us. To achieve, to win, and so on.

It is a highly emotive word. I think we're scared of it, and a bit in awe of it. But it is worth cutting it down to size. It is simply a universal feature of human relating. We're always using power – whether we want to or not.

Most importantly, we can choose *how* we use power, and *how* we are affected by the power of others.

But it's not good nor bad, and certainly not something to be feared.

Sometimes, power can be predictable. At other times, it's highly unpredictable. Think of a meeting you are involved in: it is going well, someone turns up late, the dynamics are affected, one or two challenging and unexpected questions are asked and the meeting ends in disagreement.

I wrote this short narrative about a task force I was involved in:

> *The task force included some well-known and powerful names in UK healthcare and media. This led to some constructive debates, and, occasionally, very heated arguments and conflict. Because the group came together quickly, the formal power relations were often*

poorly defined and I felt awkward, particularly given the egos in the room. There were times when I wasn't sure what my role was, for example.

There would often be unpredictable clashes and unexpected agreements. There were times when the conversation was proceeding on a predictable path and then suddenly it would spin off into a completely different area. At one meeting, I was presenting on a particular issue when the dynamics suddenly changed from a constructive debate, with useful feedback, to a completely different tack. I was feeling in control and confident and suddenly I was in despair and scrabbling to keep up.

In these sessions, conflict was very real and unpredictable. I could have taken the easy way out and kept quiet, but I continued to actively participate and put myself in the firing line.

Does that give a sense of a creative tension that was present? Again, the power was just a feature of people working together; for some there was internal panic, others were calm or even bored, and one or two were enthusiastic – all at the same time.

Pete: Yes, I really recognise the unpredictable nature of that. Power often seems to shift around the room, in really unexpected ways. The 'pecking order' or 'rank'[21] can change in real-time.

I also really notice my own contribution to this. In an earlier chapter I described how I had found myself 'pushing' a lot

---

[21] See how Arnold Mindell discusses various forms of rank, including social rank (Mindell 1992).

– mainly to no avail. That is an example of me trying to use power to get something done, but it backfiring on me.

But what is power? I think a definition might help.

Rob: Power isn't an object that one person possesses and another person doesn't. It isn't easy to quantify and fix. It is more something that emerges in relationships.

We can think about it as a way that interactions happen: for example, how one person's argument has sway over others, or how this is challenged and affected by the comments of others later on.

A nice way to think about power is as threads of elastic between people, as we all 'rub along' together[22]. As one person affects another, by a decision, action or inaction, it makes an impact on them. This in turn affects others in ways that are unknown to the originator.

This is a complex network that has both predictable and unpredictable effects on the people involved. And, it is from these interactions that decisions are taken as to what to do next.

---

[22] The sociologist Norbert Elias stresses the inadequacy of thinking of power as an object. Power is something that everyone has, sometimes without knowing it. For example, he highlights how the power a baby has over its parents is extremely strong even though she may be barely aware. He makes the case that relationships of power can be thought of as threads of elastic, or 'figuration', between people – people who are both known and unknown to us. As one person affects another, by a decision or action (or inaction), it makes an impact on them which in turn can affect others in ways that are unknown to the originator; an originator who was herself affected by the actions of others (Elias 1978).

As we have said, everyone sees things differently. Power affects that too – it depends whether you're the one with power, or not. Other people may agree who has the power, or they may not. And it can shift in a moment.

Pete: It is tempting, isn't it, to assume some people are 'leaders', with more power, and others 'followers' with less? But it is much more complex than that. The people with real power often seem to me to be in much less obvious places – like the old example of the tea-trolley-lady who knew everyone, passed on a lot of gossip, and actually had quite a lot of influence over major decisions. Despite outward appearances.

Rob: Yes, while some people may have a formal title that suggests they are the 'leader', I believe everybody leads and follows, at different times.

The CEO's *leadership* role, for example, is often thought of as providing direction to their direct reports, establishing the environment whereby people know what to do, enforcing rules, allocating resources, giving confidence to investors and to customers.

But, at the same time, the CEO is *following* others. They have to listen and respond to their shareholders, to industry regulators, to politicians, to the public, and, above all, to staff. They may be following what competitors are doing.

A middle manager may be thought of as *leading*: they are responsible for giving clarity to frontline staff, allocating resources, setting standards and so on. But they are also *following* – because they have to respond to the concerns of the public and of staff, as well as those of more senior managers.

The frontline workers are also **following** – continually adjusting their behaviour to contribute to the larger whole. To fit in with what colleagues and customers want, and to at least appear to appease or please middle and senior managers.

But they are also **leading,** when they make an ethical decision in the moment, or decide to be a role model to others. People at the interface with customers make centrally-decided policies real – or they ignore them – with every decision they make.

Which of these people have power? All of them have some, but nobody has complete power. Each person needs the cooperation of the others to achieve anything.

Pete: Of course, it is even more subtle than that, isn't it? A lot of what is going on is unnoticed, even by those involved. Most of us aren't really aware of this 'elastic' – a lot of it is unconscious.

Friendships, animosities, rivalry, envy and admiration all affect what we do and say from moment-to-moment.

We also know, from Eric Berne's 'Games People Play'[23], which popularised Transactional Analysis (Berne 2010), that we often fall into specific patterns of behaving, based on how we learnt to relate as children.

For example, I may play the rebellious 'Child' to your 'Parent'. In another situation, I may be the 'Parent' figure,

---

[23] First published in 1964.

telling you how it is. You may acquiesce, and not even quite know why you are doing so.

If this seems unlikely, try asking yourself how you behave when you are with your parents or siblings? Do you always behave like an adult, even though you are?

People fall into these roles, but so do organisations – as when a supplier interacting with a customer acts childishly, perceiving perhaps that the customer has **all** the power (often money, and access to opportunity). It usually isn't true: they may have **some** power, but not all of it.

Rob: Yes, that kind of power is rarely noticed and is therefore often not discussed.

I mentioned earlier what happens when someone new joins an organisation. Over a short period of time, a matter of weeks, what at first seemed odd or confusing becomes second nature. What to wear, the kind of language to use, what is valued and what is not, what and how to say something – it all quickly becomes 'unnoticed'.[24]

This has benefits: 'unnoticing' brings efficiency. It means we don't waste time re-writing the unofficial book on 'How we are going to work together?'. However, it does bring problems too. Invisible incumbent power may be working to limit speaking up, which limits innovation. Maybe this was what happened with Kodak?

---

[24] Bourdieu refers to this as 'habitus', whereby someone becomes experienced in the social processes of a group and can intuitively 'read' a situation in order to work out reasonable possibilities for action, yet may be unnoticing of the norms of the group (Bourdieu 1990).

This 'normalising' of power relations can happen very quickly as the infamous Stanford Prison Experiment[25] shows.

Pete: I think it is really hard to know what to do in these kinds of situations. Is it better to do or say nothing? To go along with what seems to be happening?

Rob: Or is it better to take a risk and speak up? When that might mean being ostracized.

For a business, this can mean the difference between adapting or going out of business. For some organisations this kind of dilemma can even have life and death implications – as in the case of the Bristol Royal Infirmary, which continued to perform heart surgery on very young children even though it wasn't safe (The Department of Health 2001).

Power relations had a role in that.

Pete: Yes, and given what is at stake – life, death, and businesses that fail dramatically with the loss of thousands of jobs – it is odd that power is so rarely discussed. Or, when it is, it is often seen as negative and 'Machiavellian'[26].

---

[25] In short, a group of Stanford University students were randomly split into two – half were to be prisoners, half prison warders. A mock prison block was built in the university and the prisoners remanded in custody, to be guarded by their prison warder fellow students. Respect between the two groups broke down and serious abuse occurred so quickly the experiment had to be drawn to a quick end. For more details see: http://www.prisonexp.org/psychology/2.

[26] When we read Niccolo Machiavelli's book, The Prince (Machiavelli 1984), we read a more nuanced account of power.

That doesn't really make a lot of sense, given the way we are discussing power – we all 'have' power, so surely what is important is whether we notice it and how we use it?

There are different ways to work with power, of course. Take Mary Parker Follett's idea of 'power with' (Follett 2014)[27]. She is talking, I think, about us all using our power collectively to create something valuable. This is what we nowadays call 'collaboration'.

Rob: Yes, that's a good contrast to the process where someone somehow 'orchestrates' things. In Mary Parker Follett's framing, we're all important, and results *emerge* from collaborating together, rather than being 'managed' into existence. There is no control over outcomes.

Pete: The idea of 'management' itself is a good example of the way power is exercised, isn't it? The idea suggests that everything is under control, and there is nothing to worry about. As long as everyone stays in their place, everything will be okay.

It is a story of the changing fortunes and power of the courts in 16th Century Florence, and Machiavelli's efforts to survive in the troubling waters. His 'crime' was to write it as he saw and experienced it, rather than the custom at the time to give a heroic, sugar-coated and largely fictional account of life in the court.

[27] Follett's lectures from around 1930 include such passages as: 'The individual is not a unit, but a centre of forces (both centripetal and centrifugal) and consequently society is not a collection of units, but a complex of radiating and converging, crossing and re-crossing energies. Society is a dynamic process rather than a crowd or a collection of already developed individuals'.

In theory, organisations make decisions rationally and analytically, following cold, hard facts that everyone agrees on. And managers can 'manage' the organisation and people, and somehow move them to a new place.

In practice, information is more often incomplete or unknown, some people are trustworthy, whilst others cannot be relied on. There may be personal allegiances and feuds. Greed, ego, fear and competitiveness and the desire to get one over on a rival – all come into play. This is all power at work.

Rob: There is research into this. The Danish management academic, Bent Flyvbjerg[28], worked with local politicians, town planners, the media, neighbourhood associations and several organisations in the planning, consultation and the eventual building of a bus garage (Flyvbjerg 1998 and 2001).

He explored the theory, and contrasted it with what actually happened in real life, over many years.

The project started out with a clear democratic mandate and high ideals. But it quickly became a collection of disjointed sub-projects – as the interests of a wider connected network started to become involved. There were many arguments and incidents along the way.

It wasn't that the politicians were corrupt – and neither were the government officials or suppliers incompetent.

---

[28] Flyvbjerg developed the Aristotelian idea of 'phronesis', or practical wisdom, relying on social interaction and culture within which one learns from practical engagement with the real world. Today we might speak of someone possessing wise judgment. He uses the idea to explore practical skills of power and politics.

But all the different parties involved – many of whom were claiming a democratic mandate – created a complex and unpredictable 'mess'.

The result was environmental degradation and social imbalance.

Chapter summary

— Power is not a thing. It is everywhere but is rarely noticed and even more rarely discussed.

— We all have patterns of behaviour that limit how we respond. Some of these are triggered automatically.

— It is good to notice patterns, and therefore expand our repertoire.

— These patterns are quickly normalised and become invisible. That doesn't always help.

— We can learn to speak up. But first we have to notice. And, even then, do we dare?

7 To gossip and enquire

'Pay attention to the dynamics of the relationships that you are in, how you talk, what you talk about, and the gossip you are involved in.'

Pete says: 'Information is power', isn't it? Sharing information transparently seems to me to be very important – if people had the right information then maybe better decisions would get made? Doesn't that help?

Rob replies: Well, I think it changes things. But it is hard to predict how.

First we have to consider what we mean by information. There is both formally known information, and also informal information – like gossip. If power has a bad name, give a thought to gossip!

Gossip is passed from one person to another in hushed tones, it is circulated among some people while excluding others. It spreads rapidly and virally.

Everyone knows about it, and most of us do a bit of it now and then. But we don't really give it much consideration in the way organisations work. Formal dialogue is somehow thought to be much more important.

Gossip seems to play an important role in strengthening the 'figurations of power' we talked about earlier. Minor differences are magnified, and barriers between people can grow.

This is obviously very significant – because how we see others and what we think about them affects how we hear what they say, and whether or not we act on it.

Pete: Yes, I see that. I know that a bit of whispering around the water cooler or a conversation down the pub can completely change the way what is said in a meeting is absorbed. Two people talking together may be subtly forming an alliance that other people find bewildering when they all meet later on.

This puts me in mind of some other group phenomena. Wilfred Bion[29] talked about dependency, fight/flight and pairing. These seem related to what we are describing.

In dependency, the group looks to a leader – and becomes overly dependent upon them. In fight/flight – the enemy, the source of power – is outside, and is someone to direct power against, or run away from. And, in psychological pairing, two people in a group take much of the power from the rest – who seem like inactive, disempowered bystanders by comparison.

Bion suggested that all these mechanisms, which he called 'basic assumptions', could get in the way of the group completing what he called its 'primary task' – its overt, rational purpose.

---

[29] See e.g. Whittle and Izod (2009) for an excellent summary of the practical ramifications of Bion's theories.

Rob: I think it is worth enquiring into that idea of primary task – or purpose – even further.

In my view, purpose is provisional – that is, it changes and shifts as it gets played out. No one can know the implications of having that purpose, and how it will play out as the future unfolds.

Sometimes a group becomes more cohesive over time. At other times, the group fractures. Each person is still keen to pursue the purpose as they interpret it, but it now means different things to different people.

A case in point is the schisms that have occurred in political organisations, some of the world's great religions, and even among psychologists and social scientists.

Pete: Years ago I worked for a large transnational corporation called DEC[30]. One of the core principles seemed to relate to purpose: it was 'do the right thing'.

You might hear that and think it referred to behaving ethically. But I don't think it did. It meant to do whatever was right in the situation you were in. Essentially, the principle was about trusting every one of the 120,000 employees to make their own sensible decisions about what was the right thing to do, given the prevailing conditions.

Purpose, therefore, 'emerged' after the fact, from whatever people did, and it was definitely provisional. Purpose wasn't something that was decreed on high and handed down.

---

[30] Digital Equipment Corporation, now part of HP (Schein 2003).

Of course, the company also had a formal Mission Statement. The company had a purpose, but so did every employee – and somehow we all muddled along together in what Chris Rodgers calls 'informal coalitions' (Rodgers 2007), working to meet our own needs.

Rob: Isabel Menzies-Lyth (Menzies-Lyth 1959) and her colleagues also wrote about how purpose can emerge independently of the formal purpose of an organisation. She documented how an organisation can create routines in order to meet a broader need to reduce anxiety among the people involved.

This shows how emotions and feelings can drive things in unexpected ways.

Pete: So what we are saying is that it is more about 'uncovering' organisational purpose? Finding it, rather than 'designing' it and telling people what it is.

Rob: Yes.

And I think commitment to purpose is also emergent and provisional. What I mean by that is that, if a small group of people come together and discuss their purpose, this may become the agreed purpose. But it is only provisional – it will only last as long as people continue to follow it. It is perfectly possible that people's commitment to the purpose will change over time.

In essence, we re-commit to something each time we come back into contact with the people we agreed it with. I think we re-commit by not opting out, or just by turning up.

Take our own work writing this book together. We floated the idea, and both of us agreed to write something. Then we met and looked at what we had written, and recorded some of our conversation. Then we agreed to talk on the phone. This has been going on for months – each action we have taken is a recommitment. Either of us could decide to stop but, until that happens, we are working towards a common purpose, which remains provisional.

Pete: Clarifying commitment is very important, I think. And probably the most important commitment is to staying involved even when things get difficult. They often do, when we are working with other people. Things get tricky because there are often conflicting attitudes and beliefs, and we each have our own stories about other people. These are often hard to dislodge because they relate to our identity – who we think we are.

This conversation also brings to mind certain organisational and dialogical forms, such sociocracy[31], holacracy and many others. These seem to introduce new structures and frameworks that are designed to allow people to work together better – by, for example, changing the way information is shared, purpose is clarified, and power is used.

For instance, sociocracy promotes equivalence of voice. It's not equality – where everyone has equal power. But at least everyone has a right to say what they want to say, without being shouted down.

Rob: Yes, but within those settings power can still remain 'unnoticed'.

I am not sure these approaches always guarantee a better result. For example, I had an experience of a sociocratic

---

[31] See e.g. http://sociocracy.co.uk/

type approach, where the steps were described carefully, but it missed something because we didn't pay attention to the dynamics between us. In trying to focus on the steps – and, of course, the content of the discussion we forgot the dynamics.

We became trapped by the mechanics. The person facilitating it prompted us to follow the different steps and we became fixated by them. And there was a power dynamic around the facilitator, and their knowledge of the steps, but this wasn't noticed or voiced.

Pete: That's a natural thing to some extent when you're learning something new.

Rob: Yes, but again that wasn't being discussed or brought into the room. I noticed it, and I had a sense of its effect on us, but wasn't able to voice my concern until afterwards.

Pete: I take your point. I think sociocracy, and other means of organising and making decisions, have the potential to improve how people work together. But I am not sure that they guarantee it. It still requires the individual to participate fully, and stay conscious – including of the underlying power dynamic.

I think this is also true for all the alternatives to working for traditional, hierarchical organisations that are currently being considered and reconsidered: co-operatives, networks, employee ownership, the 'Teal Organisation'[32] and so on.

---

[32] See Fred Laloux's Reinventing Organisations (2014).

Even though, in theory, you have a different kind of contract with your peers, it is still vital to participate fully – and notice what is going on in terms of power, gossip etc. I don't think any of these organisational approaches – which are sometimes tempting to see as a silver bullet – guarantee a better outcome.

They can become very 'fixed' as solutions, and that 'fixity' can get in the way of noticing. As in your example, we obsess about the 'steps' and the 'right' way to implement, at the expense of noticing and staying flexible.

Power is very elusive. It can slip away and out of sight. Noticing, and speaking up about what we notice, seems a very good move to me.

Rob: And I think when people do think about power they tend to do it in advance. So I sit there and I ask myself, how can I set up the system to enable power to be distributed or whatever? In other words, *a priori* thinking.

That is a very difficult and abstract thing to do. Because, as we have said, power relationships emerge only when we are *in* the conversation. I can do all that preparation, plan what I am going to say – and, then, half an hour later, find myself leaving a meeting having completely conceded my point.

I think a better way to deal with group dynamics of any kind is to notice them as they are happening. And, if possible, to punctuate the conversation with moments of joint reflection.

For example, I might say "I notice that each time I say something, you seem to be advocating a different position".

That may seem odd, and the other person may feel uncomfortable if the usual pattern of dialogue is disrupted in this way. But perhaps it is better than being swept along without noticing, or noticing but saying nothing?

Pete: Yes, much better. While it is tempting to come up with rules and guidelines[33] for how to do this, I don't think there are any hard and fast rules that can be applied beforehand. You have to stay aware, to notice, to be conscious. To enquire. I am suspicious of any 'Eight steps to mindfulness…' for that very reason.

This is a very **practical** wisdom – that ability to stay aware of the shifting nature of power, and to work where we have influence, rather than getting lost in our own internal process or in some theory.

It can be hard work. It can be emotionally and intellectually tiring. Sometimes it is easier just to go along with the crowd.

Rob: Thinking about things after the event doesn't always help either. In the sociocracy example I mentioned earlier, I thought about what had happened, after the session. What did I do? Well, of course, I rationalised it. Very quickly I decided that I had done the right thing, given the situation – by keeping quiet, by not speaking up.

---

[33] Bent Flyvbjerg suggests ten useful propositions (Flyvbjerg 1998). Or take, for example, Carl Rogers' 'Core Conditions' (Rogers 1967). But proclaiming these propositions is not the same as following them in practice.

My thinking about the event also became very fixed. I became certain about what had happened and what it meant. I also labelled the people involved, including myself ('not quick off the mark enough'), and moved on.

It is only in the mess of a meeting that there is real uncertainty, and therefore real choice about how to proceed. That is really where I need to enquire, in the live situation.

Pete: I suppose we can talk about it afterwards and reflect, as we are doing now, and resolve to do something different next time?

We might decide to start meetings differently. I might draw everyone's attention to power as I start the meeting. As it goes ahead, I might invite everyone to think differently, and to reflect, and to notice what's going on in terms of the power dynamics.

That's a real leadership activity – because it's an invitation for people to do something differently. To enquire into how things work in this organisation. Right here, right now.

But I may still forget to do it, in the moment!

Rob: Yes. And, if we do manage it, it's a leadership activity in the sense that there is a risk attached. For example, the fear is that the conversation may come to a point where it gets out of hand, and people might get hurt. There's also always the fear of making a mistake.

Again, of course, we can notice that, and discuss it. Someone might enquire "Why is the conversation heading in this direction?", "What are we avoiding?", "What do we fear might happen?" and so on.

Pete: I wonder if this all comes back to an underlying fear, or anxiety? I've heard people express this on many occasions in Conscious Business meetings, for example: that, ultimately, people get fired if they step out of line.

Rob: That is an extreme view of power. Most people in organisations don't get fired, do they?

Pete: I know, but other people can have an influence on your career.

Rob: And that's something to dwell on. If we enquired into it, we might realise that it is less to do with the absolute application of power – less about being sacked. And more to do with **who** is influencing your career.

There are usually many people influencing our careers. We could ask how those dynamics are having an effect on the goal we're pursuing, whether it is personal or organisational.

Pete: Yes, we can make it 'fuller' and 'broader' – we can enquire into it. Rather than narrowing it down to a single view of power as someone wielding an axe. We can enquire into it in at least three ways.

Firstly, what is happening for me? What am I really afraid of? What is that fear all about? Where does it come from?

Secondly, what is happening in the other person, or persons? Is this idea of an axe-wielding superior real? Or just some kind of fantasy or stereotype that I have?

What do they really think of me? And how could I find out? Can I simply ask?

And, thirdly, what is happening more broadly, in the group, in the context? In the setting in which I find myself? Is this a setting where some people typically have more power over others? How am I contributing to that – am I giving up my power?

We can enquire into all of this and more. I find that adopting that position of curiosity and enquiry in the moment really helps. It reduces my anxiety and I often discover something genuinely new.

Chapter summary

— Gossip has a real effect on how we perceive the world, and what happens.

— Purpose is provisional – maybe you can just 'do the right thing'?

— Systems like sociocracy and holacracy may help. But they don't guarantee anything. People still need to talk about power.

— Thinking about something in advance, and planning what to do isn't as helpful as remembering to help others notice what is happening – in real time, in the moment.

— There are at least three ways to enquire: into yourself, into what is happening with other people, and into the 'context' or dynamic.

8 The mindful leader

'Is the individual powerless? No! We can notice ourselves, guided by our emotion, and we can help others to notice too. That is leading.'

Rob says: Okay, so we have talked about how mindfulness – meaning awareness and noticing – can help us lead, especially when it gives me more freedom, more choice.

We've talked about groups, and how they are a major impact on our working lives, and the importance of noticing power.

Living entirely alone certainly doesn't seem like a good option! But what about the personal, the individual?

How do I orient myself within a group? How do I know if I am doing the right thing? And when I feel outnumbered or a bit battered in a group, what can I rely on?

Pete replies: Yes, just because the group is powerful, does that mean I am powerless? I really hope not.

But what does it mean to be personally powerful? And what might I use that power to do? What am I 'motivated' to do[34]?

Rob: Sometimes going along with the group may be the best thing. Perhaps we might be able to align our motives and purpose with what is happening in the group, to fit in?

But that idea brings us into tension immediately with our own individual sense of purpose and getting our own individual needs met.

Some cultures believe that the individual comes first, has more power, more rights. Some that society has more power, and we should do our best to fit in. But, whichever it is, there does seem to be a role for the individual.

Pete: Personal confidence also seems to be a central issue for leaders. For example, young business people are repeatedly told that they must 'be confident'. Personal confidence and 'drive' are seen as a sure route to 'success'.

---

[34] The central idea of individual motivation – and needs – is everywhere in the literature around business, management and organisations. It is the central plank of the human relations movement – in stark contrast to the idea of people as cogs in a machine. Take a look at the work of: Elton Mayo, known for the 'Hawthorne' studies which suggested that people modify their behaviour in response to being observed; Kurt Lewin: a pioneer in the areas of social, organizational, and applied psychology; Abraham Maslow: best known for creating 'Maslow's hierarchy of needs'. Daniel Goleman, with his work on emotional intelligence (Goleman 2009), popularised the idea of us as human beings, with motivations, drives and emotions. And apparently we even have the right to be happy at work according to psychologists like Martin Seligman (Seligman 2002) and economists like Richard Layard.

'Traditional leaders' project confidence. They know what is right, and they show the rest of us the way. Some might call this being 'assertive', but I think that would be a mistake.

We're redefining leadership as helping others to notice, to become more aware. Not to tell others what to do, or how to behave.

Rob: Let's start with motivation. Can we notice it, and be mindful of it?

Pete: I think motivation is too big a construct. It includes too many ideas. What I find, personally, is that I can notice my feelings. This is not easy, and I need to remind myself to slow down, if I am to notice them properly.

I can also notice my thoughts, my levels of energy – the general state I am in. I can certainly notice when I am attracted towards certain things, people, or ideas. Or when I need to get away. I guess I would call these values and maybe instincts.

A lot of it is 'relational'. I can notice what I think about other people, and try to remember that it may just be a story I am making up. Even though it may seem very real to me.

I can also notice and enquire into the patterns – what stays the same, or recurs. And I can notice the changes too. At times, I may feel buoyed up and ready to take on the world. At other times, I feel flat and disheartened and ready to give up.

Rob: Yes, I think we all experience ups and downs in our motivation. Sometimes this is personal, and individual. Our motivations and moods shift all the time.

Sometimes it is about the group we are in. Being in a great group, or with great colleagues, can be very motivating, very exciting. Or it can be pressurising.

But how do people keep going when the group is against them? When the only apparent way forward means standing out from the crowd, being different?

Pete: I don't know. It sometimes seems quite miraculous. But I think there are several important steps. The first is to become more aware. If we are so busy running around that we never take time to slow down and just notice, it is hard to be aware.

To be mindful, we need to reflect, and we need to enquire.

Taking the time to really listen to what other people are trying to tell us is also very helpful. How often do we just say 'yes, yes' and get straight on with the next thing?

Being more aware is the first part of what Carl Rogers called congruence (Rogers 1967) – it is one of the 'core conditions'. Becoming aware of what is going on inside oneself. Feelings, thoughts, instincts, motives, dreams, hopes, aspirations and so on.

The second part of congruence is the art of responding to what is happening. What I mean by that is that, as we experience all that is happening to us, including what is internal, and what is coming in from outside through our senses, we have the option to 'go with it'. Or not.

Reacting is one thing, responding is another. The latter has a sense of conscious choice.

For example, I guess we have all had the experience of sitting in a meeting and suddenly feeling the desire to say a particular thing. For me, this starts somewhere in my body and rises up to a point where sometimes it is bursting to get out.

Now, at that point, I have a choice. I can either deliberately suppress the idea, and let the moment pass. Or I may choose to verbalise the idea. Or I may decide to sit with the feeling, and explore it.

Of course, I can't consciously do any of these if I don't notice the feeling in the first place. But, if I notice it I have a choice.

It doesn't have to be something I say. I might feel a strong desire to get up and leave. I can choose to follow that desire. Or not. To suppress it.

This kind of congruence – responding to, and 'making real' what we feel and experience – may perhaps be better moderated by two of Rogers' other core conditions: empathy and unconditional positive regard (which we might more simply call 'respect').

Sometimes staying in the meeting or staying quiet may be the right thing to do to maintain or develop relationships. This is not about just giving you access to my stream of consciousness!

Rob: It strikes me that there is a lot of uncertainty attached to what you are describing. When that happens for me, and I choose one route or another, I really don't know what is going to happen next. I find relaxing into that and trusting my 'inner elephant'[35] very helpful.

Learning to tolerate this uncertainty[36] is, for me, an important part of leadership. Acting from that position of not knowing the outcome, being in the state of enquiry, is the very essence of leading.

We might also call it 'holding'. That term is often used to refer to a facilitator holding a space in which, for example, a group can reflect on its own dynamic. But I am using it to refer to holding my own personal process. As with a group, I let whatever wants to happen happen, and I allow myself to reflect and enquire into what is happening.

This is what social scientists call reflexivity[37].

Pete: Yes, that is a great way to put it. The essence of it is letting whatever happens happen, not pushing for what we want.

By the way, I think people sometimes misunderstand assertiveness and think it means 'getting our own way'. One of the implications of understanding the world in the way we are describing it – as a world of little certainty, where we can't hope for control – is that many times we

---

[35] From Jonathan Haidt comes the idea of us as a rider on an elephant – the rider may think they are in control, but really only the elephant knows where it is going (Haidt 2006).

[36] Karl Weick pays attention to questions of ambiguity and uncertainty in his work on sense-making (e.g. Weick 1995).

[37] Reflexivity is the idea that our awareness, thoughts and actions can come back to influence us – in other words, an awareness bending back on itself.

won't get our own way. Whatever we do, things may work out differently from how we hope and expect. Instead we have to 'go with the flow'.

But that doesn't mean that we can't assert our own views. Assertiveness is about letting others understand your needs. If you do this without aggression, and also without passive aggression[38], there is perhaps a reasonable chance that you'll get those needs met, given our common desire to help our fellows.

But you can't guarantee it. Control is a form of aggression and, in my view, just as likely to backfire as not.

One very simple technique for expressing needs is to use an I-statement, or I-message[39]. This means simply stating what you need, value, believe, or feel in the form 'I [verb] [such-and-such]'.

For example, 'I need a break', which is different from 'Now we'll take a break' or even 'Let us take a break'.

This kind of approach – followed by an enquiry, such as "What do you think?" – allows us to clearly state a position, but still stay open to what others may want. It avoids us falling back into the need for control.

Rob: The other thing I notice is that, often, when I decide to speak up in a meeting, I may also notice my own fears

---

[38] Passive aggression is expressing hostility indirectly – for example, by procrastinating, being stubborn, or sulking; or deliberately (perhaps unconsciously) failing to do a task for which you have accepted responsibility.

[39] This was an idea developed by Thomas Gordon, an associate of Carl Rogers (Bolton 2011). Another example might be 'I feel angry'.

and doubts. What if what I am about to say doesn't go down well? What if my well-intentioned intervention – designed to help get the project back on track, or whatever it is – just makes everyone angry and causes a huge storm, a huge firefight?

Pete: I have learnt that one way to handle that is to be congruent about those 'secondary' feelings, even as they arise. In the here and now. I might say, for example, "I have something to say which the rest of you may find very upsetting, and I am worried about hurting anyone". **Before** I launch in with whatever I have to say.

Of course, there is a huge range of ways to express what we need to say, once we reach that choice point. We can stay quiet and take our feelings elsewhere for processing.

Or we can get angry, thump the table, threaten, shout, whisper, give a meaningful look, make a hurtful aside, wheedle and complain, or simply storm out, slamming the door.

I find two things helpful in making that choice about what to do or say. The first is to consider the impact on the other people. I can enquire into what may be going on for them. This is empathy – putting myself in the other person's shoes and trying to see the world as they see it.

Maybe they said something that triggered my need to speak? Maybe they said something that I felt hurt by? But maybe they had, in turn, been hurt by some other event that I know nothing of?

Maybe this possibility will help me to remember they are a person, like me, and deserve my respect – even if it is only for having been human, and made a mistake?

Rob: Yes, simply asking myself "Would I want someone to say that to me?" often helps me decide whether to speak up or not.

Pete: The other thing I can enquire into is what is happening in the room, in the group. As we said in the last chapter, there are always other things going on, much of which is beneath the surface.

By this I mean power, and other facets of the group dynamic, and I also mean projection and transference[40].

It is all too easy, when things aren't going well, and we might be experiencing feelings of incompetence, to ***project*** these feelings onto another person. To perhaps look for things in another person to confirm our diagnosis that they are lazy or incompetent. When, all along, we are really worried about these attributes in ourselves.

As I said before, it is also quite common to meet someone who reminds of us of someone else we knew, perhaps in childhood. It is always then possible that we will start to treat them as we treated the other person.

When I label someone else as lazy, I may be talking about myself. And I may also be talking about what is happening in the group. Perhaps the group is being a bit lazy – in its thinking, for example.

---

[40] See, for example, the wonderful work of Irvin Yalom on groups (e.g. Yalom and Leszc 2008).

Groups are complex, and do seem to have a life of their own.

Projection and transference are very common, and perhaps the best way to deal with them is to notice them, to become aware of them. To see them as normal, but temporary. As we do so, we regain choice.

Rob: That sounds easy, but it can be very difficult, can't it?

Because, firstly, these things may often be unconscious – we may not notice that we are doing them, or that they are happening. And, secondly, perhaps we don't want to bring them into our awareness because they are linked to difficult emotions and feelings.

If I can't handle the feelings that come with thinking I am incompetent or lazy, it is probably easier for me to think one of my colleagues is.

Pete: Yes, it is difficult. Let me give you another example.

I guess it has happened to us all: someone says or writes something about us that seems very hurtful. Once a client said something about me in an email to me that I was personally appalled by. I felt ashamed, really sad, disappointed – like I had let everyone down, including myself. I felt my self-image, my pride in my skills, had been permanently punctured.

The only problem was I didn't really know I felt those things. Because my first reaction when I read the message was to feel really angry instead. In my anger I wrote back and started making demands: that he retract what he had said. That he think seriously about what he had said, reconsider and reflect.

I also thought that his way of saying it – by email – was wrong, and I was angry because he hadn't even had the courage to say this to me face-to-face. I thought he was putting me in a box, telling me what he thought rather than trying to find out what was really going on for me, and I had all sorts of other complaints about him too.

It was only as I reflected, with the help of a friend, that I started to see that my reaction was just that – a reaction. I had reacted without really delving into what was going on for me. As I started to see beyond the anger, and started to feel my way into those feelings, new thoughts emerged.

Maybe, just maybe, there was something deeper going on here? Was this a pattern? Is there a part of me that is easily hurt by just this kind of thing? Am I overly sensitive to exactly that kind of statement – to being punctured in that way? Not because the other person said it, but because of what it meant to me. Was I constructing my own meaning, a meaning very different from what was intended?

After a while, I began to see that there were alternative interpretations of what had been said. Maybe it was a fairly innocent, off-the-cuff remark, sent in haste? And the real problem was my reaction?

Does that make sense?

Rob: Yes. And did you notice that all the things you said in your replies were useful advice to you, not to your client? To reflect more? To talk to yourself face-to-face, courageously? To try to find out what was really going on for you?

Pete: I did, eventually.

A psychologist friend told me a decade or more ago that what we say to and about others is often really directed towards ourselves. More and more I see truth in this. Sometimes all we need to do to unpick difficult situations is listen really carefully to what we are saying, or, more likely, tempted to say, to others.

Anyway, I realised the real work I needed to do was internal – not in dialogue with my client. Not trying to argue or prove my point. But to enquire into what was happening for me. The history, of course, but also the patterns that remain. Who I am today – how I habitually behave. How I see the world.

It is only by understanding this that I might be able to introduce a bit more choice – and respond rather than react, the next time something like that happens.

Rob: It is a good example. I think it is really worth trying to separate our projections from reality.

Pete: Most of us are lazy or incompetent some of the time. Pretending we are not – or making ourselves or the other person into a saint – is just another projection.

A better approach is to try to get a clearer view of the current reality. And that means noticing how our own individual perceptions – our own projections and transference – can get in the way.

I can also ask "What did this person actually do that upset me, or made me think they were lazy?". What did I actually observe, versus what I imagine?

I don't think it is easy to do this, but I do think the brain is 'plastic' (Siegel 2010), and even old dogs can learn new tricks. This means that leading mindfully includes being committed to enquiring into how we see the world, and actively updating ourselves by, for example, trying to get past, or at least become aware of, our cognitive biases, and our unconscious material.

Chapter summary

— Am I powerless? – No, not at all. Mindfulness is a choice.

— Try following your inner 'elephant'. (Or elephants. There may be more than one!)

— Being aware of your feelings – how you label them, and responding to what is 'coming up for you' – is very important. This increases **'choice'**.

— Learn to speak up – there are ways to be more honest and transparent without hurting others.

— Living is relational – projection and transference, for example, are very common. Try to notice them. And remember the stories we tell about other people.

9 Noticing, naming and holding

'Purpose sustains itself by continual challenge. Building self-esteem is an inner journey. And there is always value in not knowing.'

Rob says: We spoke a little about group purpose. But does the idea of individual purpose help, do you think?

Pete replies: Perhaps. I suppose if am aware of my purpose I can try to follow it. The same goes for my values – presumably I can make a choice whether to follow them or not?

If I value honesty, then many times during a day I may be faced with opportunities to be honest. In every conversation, I can choose the level of honesty I apply.

Shall I be honest that I am disappointed by the way a project is going? Or shall I adapt what I say to please other people and to get another of my values met – like the need for recognition?

I think values, like purpose, come and go. They are dynamic not fixed, and depend to some extent on the relationships we are in. So we are best served by trying to notice how they are right now, and adapting to them –

rather than having a fixed idea of what they should or could be.

Rob: Stafford Beer talked in terms of POSIWID, meaning 'the Purpose Of a System Is What It Does' (Beer 2009). This suggests that purpose is an emergent property of a relational system, rather than simply being located in an individual.

If you spend a little time noticing, you'll probably quickly notice that purpose changes. It develops from day to day, hour to hour, minute to minute and even second to second.

If I am eating lunch with a friend, my purpose is probably something to do with enjoying the food and conversation. Or maybe I am trying to get something across, or share something, or get some support.

At a business meeting an hour later, my purpose might be different. I may be trying to build a very different kind of relationship. Purpose is arising from the context.

So, instead of a long search for personal purpose, as if it is a pot of gold at the end of a rainbow, I suggest simply noticing. Noticing what you do and how you do it. Noticing while we are acting, and letting that awareness influence how we respond – in other words, being reflexive.

Pete: Reflexivity really is one of those difficult ideas.

I develop a sense of purpose in my mind, but it is elusive and not yet fully formed. I find it hard to describe to others. But, as I take action, I start to become clearer. I start to find ways to describe my (or our) purpose to myself and others.

Rob: In other words, it is an iterative, recursive process that combines thought, feeling and practice.

The image that appears often in mythology is of a snake eating its own tail.

Pete: All of that said, I think there are often tensions. Between a long-standing sense of purpose – to do or achieve something – and what happens in my daily interactions with people.

I may be able to see a pattern in my purpose and in what I value. My need to feed and clothe and educate my children does not go away. Nor does my desire to help people build purposeful businesses.

Sometimes this purpose is in harmony with my daily interactions with people, and sometimes they clash. It is in those clashes that I notice I sometimes shift my patterns of thought, only slightly perhaps, but a shift nonetheless. This is when I've seen my thoughts develop.

When that happens, I really think it is worth stopping, and taking time to reflect on this difference.

I can ask myself "What does it mean when my instincts and what I am feeling seem to conflict with what I sense or feel the group wants?".

Rob: Of course, there's another challenge: actually following your purpose and living your values. Groups and our relationships with other people can distract us from our individual purpose.

But they can also be very helpful. If we work in groups with high levels of trust, we can all hold each other to account on our purpose. Other people can remind us of our commitments, even if they slip from our own consciousness.

It seems that both the individual and the group are important. And the tensions between them are important too.

This and other paradoxes seem to keep coming up in our conversation.

Pete: Yes, I noticed that too.

My experience of leading is that it is full of paradoxes. We have to do things fast, but we also have to go slow – if we are to listen properly, and make wise decisions. We are trying to please all the stakeholders, **and** ourselves, all at the same time.

Facing a paradox can feel really uncomfortable. Either I want to get away. Or I want to eliminate it. Sometimes I want to ignore it.

But, rather than 'resolving' a paradox – in the sense of fixing it, or finding a way through it – I think a more useful process may be to live with it. Be with the paradox. That sounds very 'Zen', I know.

Rob: It doesn't need to be mystical. I think 'being with it' simply means not doing any of the things you describe – not running away, or getting rid of it. It means just sitting with the discomfort, the difficult feelings. Perhaps enquiring into them.

This is one way to 'hold'. To create a container for the feelings.

Another thing we can do is 'name' it. So a leadership behaviour might be to say 'I see a paradox here. On the one hand, X. And, on the other hand, Y. The two together seem to form a paradox. They're contradictory and there's no obvious solution.'

That person might then leave it up to others to take the next step. This is a particular kind of leadership – one that involves facilitating a process, and getting out of the way. There's no attempt to change things.

This approach is hard for many traditional leaders to adopt, because 'changing things' is often how they reached the positions they are in.

Pete: Yes, the conventional view of leadership seems to require that I know the way forward, whereas I think I am more comfortable with 'not knowing' and letting things emerge.

I think it is also useful to consider different ways to lead depending on what the context is: my role, my position in the organisation, and my relationships with others.

I think everyone leads.

Front-line employees *lead* by doing their best to meet the needs of those immediately around them: their clients, their colleagues. They may lead by making suggestions and starting initiatives that turn the organisation in a particular direction.

Managers *lead* by organising the efforts of a group of employees to meet the needs of clients, colleagues etc. They coach and support. And, if they wish, they can help other people's initiatives gain momentum.

More senior managers *lead* by looking more broadly, across the piece. If they are wise, they also set an example – in how they communicate, and how they listen. Their 'not knowing' can create a space for growth and development.

Rob: What about 'transformational' managers? I keep hearing that term these days.

Pete: Yes, it's fashionable isn't it, to talk of transformation?

I think managers who seek to transform are *leading* by enquiring into the bigger picture, and by trying to ensure that the organisation has the right kind of leadership. That means leaders with the right communication skills, but also, as Bill Tate (Tate 2012) wisely points out, creating the right context for leadership to operate well.

Leading isn't something people do alone. The organisational context makes it easier or harder.

Transformational leadership also means understanding the broader market the organisation fits into. In the 'market', we include customers, potential customers, people who will never be customers, suppliers, partners, influencers, media, regulators, employees and potential and future employees.

Awareness grows to encompass a pretty large field. And the transformational leader's job is to bring that awareness into everyday conversations with the people they serve.

Rob: Everybody is leading, and they may all be acting in service of some kind of shared group purpose, as well as their own. All of these people can notice and point out 'difference' – of opinion, of perspective and so on.

Of course, 'levels of leadership' are imaginary. Each of us can also operate in any role. It is only our thinking, and the way we perceive the power of those around us, that constrains us.

What, for example, would happen if a person who works on the frontline in a big corporation started looking at the bigger picture for the organisation – what it might be trying to achieve strategically?

Senior management might laugh or snub that person.

But, actually, a wise management team might see the value of having that kind of strategic thinking at the frontline of the organisation. After all, senior managers are usually very cut off from the reality of work, and may be the worst people to be 'setting' strategy.

Pete: For me, whoever is leading, the approach to leadership is more about facilitating – about noticing, and getting out of the way – than stepping into the breach waving a flag, and saying 'follow me!'.

It's probably a personal thing, and I think there is room for different kinds of leadership at different times.

My guess is that the facilitative approach requires at least as much courage, if not more, than the conventional model. Because, apart from anything else, we don't recognise that paradigm of leadership so easily.

Rob: That's right, the kind of post-conventional leadership we are describing is less well known. There is talk these days of the anti-heroic leader[41]. But, it seems to me, that even this kind of leader – the leader who facilitates and supports, and points out difference – is fairly heroic.

Pete: Yes, I think it is an inner journey more than an external one, and that takes real courage. As we have said, a very important thing is to notice one's self, one's own emotion, one's own ways of relating to others, one's own ways of approaching problems.

We all have the ability to look inwards, I believe. But few choose to do it. Staying busy and distracted is far easier.

Rob: Why is it so difficult to look inside, and talk about what we see?

Pete: I think it is, at least in part, because our families and our education system discourage it.

Jesper Juul (Juul 1995), for example, points out that our education system, and a lot of parenting, is designed to reward behaviour, not reflection.

This, by the way, has the effect of building self-confidence. If you praise someone for speaking up well in class, or for giving a good presentation at work, they will learn to repeat

---

[41] E.g. The Anti-hero Project
http://www.cloresocialleadership.org.uk/Richard-Wilson.aspx

that behaviour. They will become more confident as a speaker, or as a presenter.

But perhaps feeling good about our behaviour – having self-confidence – isn't the same as having good self-esteem? Self-esteem, to me, is more about how we value 'our whole selves', not just our behaviour.

Good self-esteem is important if we are to look inside and discover what is there.

Carl Rogers, among others, was also keen that we distinguish the 'person' from the behaviour, perhaps for this very reason.

Think about it: a person who is confident in their skills will cope very well when the task is the same task – giving another presentation. But they may really struggle when the task is new – and their skill level is low.

At these times, we talk of having '*inner* confidence' – or self-esteem – to cope with the uncertainty, the 'not knowing', about how it will work out.

Attachment theory (Bowlby 2008) suggests that what happens in early life can affect all this.

But I also believe that noticing and awareness give us the opportunity to build our own self-esteem. To learn to accept and appreciate our inner selves, regardless of how well or badly we do things, and regardless of how we were parented.

Rob: Yes, self-esteem is really important because it also allows us to cope with the complexity of real-life situations, where we really cannot know what the outcome is going to be.

None of us can predict the effect of saying one thing or another in a conversation. We have to rub along together, and take the rough with the smooth.

It means feeling difficult feelings if someone in a group 'attacks' us, and still 'holding' that conversation.

It requires 'holding the space' when we name a paradox, or point out different ways of perceiving the world.

It means managing myself.

Pete: Yes, to me that is the essence of leading. It is about being able to 'hold the space', and continue to notice, even when the conversation gets very hot. It is about ***not*** knowing the answer, about being able to tolerate difficult feelings and emotions, mainly our own.

It is about being able to notice and allow purpose to emerge from the group. So, rather than me working out what my purpose is and forcing it on to you, I let a group purpose emerge.

Mary Parker Follett highlighted the value, and the difficulty, of doing this, when she spoke about the idea of finding the 'collective will'[42]. It is wonderful when it happens but it is not easy to do.

---

[42] Mary Parker Follett: "Many people talk as if the collective will were lying around loose to be caught up whenever we like, but the fact is we must go to our group and see that it is brought into existence" (Héon et al. 2014).

If I remember, I can ask Stafford Beer's 'POSIWID' question in the context of the group. "What is our purpose?", "What are we doing?", "What is emerging right now?".

Frameworks and questions[43] can help. But, really, this is all about noticing – sensing and enquiring into what is happening in the group – which takes us right back to what we discussed in the last chapter. Power, and what is happening more systemically.

I think this is what Mary Parker Follett, at the beginning of the 20th century, and Dan Siegel, at the beginning of the 21st, mean when they talk of integration.

Rob: Another very popular word. But what does it mean exactly?

Pete: As we notice what is happening in the group, we notice difference. Difference between levels, difference between values, different roles, different purposes, different perceptions. In modern terms, we might imagine this happening at different neurological levels in our brains.

Occasionally, something almost magical happens, when these differences become clear. One person says something, another something else. If we 'hold' all these then, somehow, sometimes, a third, quite different position appears.

This is not a compromise, but something new that genuinely arises from the group – something we can genuinely commit to.

---

[43] For example, The Blueprint for Better Business
http://www.blueprintforbusiness.org/

This is easier to understand, I think, if we think in terms of dynamic relationships between people – rather than static objects and things. New perceptions, new perspectives and new relationships are formed through the process of conflict.

Somehow, overall, there is more integration than before.

That leads to other enquiries, such as "What is the next step?", "What do we need to do next?", "How would we go about that?", and perhaps "Who needs to be involved?".

In short, we can keep enquiring.

Rob: It really matters *how* I say all this, doesn't it? How I make these enquiries?

I am always looking for a balance between being assertive, and being humble. Humbly listening, really enquiring, and being open – and then asserting my position again. And so on.

Pete: And one's attitude is really important. I think of attitude as the 'angle' from which I see something. If my personal stories are negative, then I will see one thing. If they are more positive, more constructive, more appreciative, then I'll see another.

Rob: I also need to be humble in the sense of realising that I may not get my ideas across. It may not be the right time, or there may be a thousand other reasons why it won't work to speak up.

In that case, I hope I'll always remember what WC Fields said: 'If at first you don't succeed, try, try, try again. Then quit. There's no point in being a damn fool about it.'

Chapter summary

— Purpose and values are not fixed: they depend on the situation, and they change over time.

— Conventional leadership is about saying 'follow me'. Another way to lead is to 'facilitate' – to allow whatever is emerging to emerge. Both are valid, depending on the situation.

— It's important to distinguish behaviour from the person. We all make mistakes. 'To err is human'.

— Discovering self-esteem is an inner journey, and essential for dealing with uncertainty.

— Mindful, or conscious, leadership means noticing, helping others to notice, holding a space, and enquiring. This may help with the process of integrating differences.

10 Practice - for the individual

'Try some practices for individuals: try meditating, writing and, above all, slowing down to listen.'

Rob says: Russell Ackoff, a life-long investigator of organisational life, made the following observation of the challenges we face (Ackoff 1979):

> *'[We] are not confronted with problems that are independent of each other, but with dynamic situations that consist of complex systems of changing problems that interact with each other. I call such situations messes. ... [We] do not solve problems, [we] manage messes'.*

I think we sometimes forget this. And, sometimes, we don't realise this in the first place, so we seek straightforward solutions. We think that we can find a quick fix to a problem, without realising that the situation is a 'mess'. It has wider connections and implications, and these have consequences – both opportunities and threats.

Pete replies: Yes, it would be nice, wouldn't it, if life was simple and, having described the situation in terms of its symptoms, we could then go on and prescribe a medicine to sort it out. But I suppose it is a bit like Eastern medicine:

we are saying that the body and mind, and indeed the whole of our lives, need to be treated as an interconnected whole. And, therefore, we can't just pop a pill to fix it.

I think what we can do is introduce some tools and techniques that not everyone may be aware of. And, maybe, explain how we think it is best to employ them.

Rob: Yes, and the focus does need to be on applying these tools and techniques properly and over time. Again, using your medical analogy, if a doctor prescribes diet and exercise, it is unlikely to have much effect unless the patient actually makes the changes required, and sustains them for a reasonable amount of time.

We are often talking about changing habits, including some mental habits that probably need to be challenged.

The first of these, for me, is postponing judgement and enabling new connections to be made. I think we all have a tendency to rush in and 'decide'. We see a situation or learn something new and, partly because of the hurly-burly of life, we expect to find a 'quick fix'.

I think, instead, it is more useful to learn to notice something – a change of situation perhaps – and mull it for a while. Sometimes, when we look at things over and over, or just very carefully, we notice new aspects that we hadn't noticed at first glance.

Pete: Is it unfair to attribute some of that rush to the advertising and media that fills our lives? Much advertising seems to peddle the idea that, if I buy the product, it will quickly fix my problem. The emphasis being on the simplicity of the problem – and speed of the cure.

But, as we have repeatedly said, life is more complex than that.

Slowing down, and postponing judgement so we can examine all the ramifications of the situation, is a really good habit to get into. Call it contemplation if you will. Or we might call it 'slow thinking'.

I think it is also vital to include the views of others as we do that. Personally, I find my thinking can get very stuck in particular loops. But, when I enter into a dialogue with another person, then my thinking can change profoundly.

For that to happen, though, I need to really listen. As organisational psychologist Chris Argyris reputedly said "We don't listen, we reload". Much of the time, our brains are getting a riposte ready, or simply continuing on our existing train of thought, rather than actually listening to what another person is saying.

Learning to listen properly is also difficult because we have to open ourselves up to the possibility we are wrong. We need to become 'vulnerable'.

For many people, being convinced they are right is a cornerstone of their life. Being open can be emotionally upsetting – emotions may arise that we are not used to or ready for. But I think we have to be prepared to tip up that particular applecart if we are to really listen, and really learn.

Rob: Yes, and part of the challenge is to create a space that is safe enough for that kind of careful listening and slow thinking to go on. When people really listen and think slowly, then there will also be enquiry – people will start to ask questions from a position of real curiosity.

Real curiosity is different from pretending to listen. I have met professional listeners who have forgotten the art of listening, the art of really being curious, of enquiring.

Some people also ask questions but with a hidden point to get across. Rhetorical questions of any kind aren't about being curious – they are a form of advocating.

Pete: And sometimes people don't ask questions at all. Instead we all 'mind-read' sometimes – guessing what other people are thinking or feeling, and failing to check. It's risky because the hidden assumptions never get exposed.

Rob: Yes, the other thing that is really helpful in dialogue is the idea that it is okay to challenge assumptions.

That means firstly noticing any assumptions that are being made. For example, who is controlling things, who is setting the agenda? All the power relations we mentioned earlier. What are the 'patterns'? Does one person always take a superior role, and another inferior, for example?

And, then, being able to challenge these. Having some language that makes it okay to point out the assumption, and question it, and whether or not it is helpful.

I'd like to talk about some of the tools and techniques that we have personally found useful in helping us navigate this more complex world. I'd like to mention some – like writing, and action learning.

Pete: Yes, but before we get into specifics, I think there are a couple of other important things to point out.

The first is that, for me, all these techniques are really facets of the same process. They just highlight different features that different people have found useful. The best thing is to explore different techniques to try to find a few that really work for you.

There are so many brilliant people who have developed theories[44] and techniques[45] to explore. We can't even begin to mention them all here, but, hopefully, we can offer a few starting points.

The second thing I want to mention, again, are Carl Rogers' 'core conditions' (Rogers 1967). There's a risk, when we pick up a 'technique', that we may start to use it while forgetting the underlying humanity – and humility – that all such approaches need and require.

I think *how* we follow the technique or the process is just as important, if not more important, than the process itself. Especially when we are focusing on the relationships we are trying to build.

---

[44] Two people who are really worth exploring, if you want to find more about the underpinning of these kinds of approaches, are John Dewey (Dewey 2007), the US pragmatist philosopher and educationalist, writing in the early twentieth century; and Kurt Lewin, the psychologist who, following the Second World War, developed action research and other approaches which help people learn together.

[45] Some other great people to explore: SH Foulkes (Foulkes 1983), Bill Torbert (Torbert 2004) and Ken Gergen (Gergen 2009).

Rob: I also believe these core conditions – empathy, respect and congruence – are really helpful as a set of systemic conditions to put in place as we practise these techniques.

Pete: Yes, just to recap – and making it very simple – there are, as you say, three core conditions:

Empathy, which can be understood as the process of putting ourselves in another's shoes, of trying to see the world through their eyes, to even feel what they may feel[46].

Unconditional positive regard ('respect') is the idea that, even when we are less than happy with another person's behaviour – what they say or do – we remind ourselves of their essential humanity. Their right, exactly like our own, to exist, to be human, to make mistakes and learn and grow.

The last one, ***congruence***, is a way of being: a way of being aware of ourselves and what is happening to us and others. And being transparent and open about that.

The 'trick' is to be transparent while also balancing the other two core conditions – so that we say something helpful for ourselves and other people. If we can empathise, and consider another person's essential humanity when we speak up, this becomes possible.

Rob: I think it is also very important to remember to apply these core conditions to ourselves. For example, when we

---

[46] Research on e.g. mirror neurons suggests this may physically be possible. See e.g. https://www.youtube.com/watch?v=Tq1-ZxV9Dc4 and https://www.youtube.com/watch?v=CnvSRvmRlgA

learn, we throw ourselves open. As we said, this can feel difficult, scary even.

If I can remember to be empathic towards myself – to remember I am human, that I am a learning being, that I have feelings and can be hurt as well as safe – then that may help me be more honest with myself. And, ultimately, over time, build a better relationship with myself.

Pete: For me, that also includes remembering to have fun with all these techniques. Learning can be fun and enjoyable – it can be a great source of richness in many ways.

Rob: Okay, now we have discussed the context, let me say that something I particularly enjoy is writing, and helping other people to write. In particular, I have seen many people helped by writing narratives of striking events in their working lives.

What I usually do is ask people to write a short narrative about what happened. This could include moments of tension or an argument, or it could be a discussion when something unexpected emerged. It might be an event that was puzzling – where there was no obvious easy outcome or solution.

Pete: Sounds good. Tell me more.

Rob: Well, the first thing is to write quite soon after the event. This minimises post-hoc rationalisation. It allows you to include all the muddling and conflict that you notice before these all fade in the process of making sense of the situation. Over time, emotions and feelings are lost and become secondary to the 'story'. Our aim is to include all that messiness – including how it all feels.

These narratives don't need to be long – a few hundred words is fine.

They are usually best written in the first person, making yourself the central character. 'I did this... ', 'I said that...'.

It isn't about the quality of the writing – this isn't an English exam. It is just about capturing what happened in as much of its complexity as you can.

Once you have written the narrative, there are several options. You can take the narrative to an 'action learning set', or a group of trusted friends, and read your account out loud. I find reading out loud helps because people sense your emotion better. They may then notice things about your story that will be new to you. Even the act of reading it aloud seems to increase awareness.

Another option is to leave the narrative for a couple weeks. This is the basis of writing a journal – which I think is also a really useful practice. When you come back to the text a couple of weeks later, you may notice things quite differently. Events that seemed puzzling at the time may now have run their course, and you can try and reconcile the confusion of the moment with the clarity of hindsight.

And in doing this, you can play over in your mind how you might have acted differently.

When I do this with groups, I often encourage the participants to redraft their accounts along the way – after they have had feedback from the other participants, for example. This is a good way to integrate any new insights.

It gives something to refer back to, and see how your practice is changing over time. New 'relationships' are also formed – people's perceptions of the issues, and of each other, change and develop.

Pete: That's a great technique. One of the things I like about it is how simple it is. You just need a pen and paper, a bit of time, and preferably some colleagues or friends to share it with.

I sometimes use mind maps – to see what is happening in a particular situation. It helps me to 'pile up' the events and to be able 'to look them over'. Perhaps I will notice a sequence or a pattern. Or at least I have the satisfaction of off-loading my thoughts onto paper.

But I think writing a fuller narrative is a great idea because I think we reveal a lot more of what is happening unconsciously that way.

I think this is also part of the appeal of many meditative or 'mindfulness' practices. Over time, if we meditate, we start to notice what is less conscious, less obvious. It is a bit like simply looking at something, or trying to draw or paint it.

To look and draw and paint we have to learn to really **see** what is there, and I think meditative practices of all kinds help with this.

Rob: Does it have to be a formal process?

Pete: For me, meditation really just means sitting. I find that incredibly difficult to do in my busy world. My life is so structured and busy, with work, family, friends etc – I find it hard to give space to meditation. Whenever I might have a moment – sitting on the train, for example – it is so easy to fill up that little space with looking at my phone, checking my email, or a million and one other distractions.

I was initially attracted to Martin Boroson's One Moment Master (Boroson 2007) for that very reason – it's a programme that allows for meditation in just 60 seconds!

But really I have found the most useful thing to do is to break the habit of filling all my available time with activity. Perhaps the easiest way into this is to simply try to sit still for a few minutes.

How long can I do this? Before the urge to move, to read a newspaper, to turn on the TV, to listen to something, arises? I know for myself, I feel these urges almost straight away. My head fills with things I 'should' be doing.

What I try to do when that happens is simply notice these urges. It sometimes feels a little, or even very, uncomfortable. Or sometimes it feels somewhere in between. Not really uncomfortable and yet not quite comfortable either.

Whatever happens I try to stay sitting and simply notice the discomfort. Simply noticing what arises.

After a while I might notice my 'trying'. How it is 'important' for me to 'succeed', how important it is to me to complete the time I have allotted to this activity. To not give up.

If that happens, I just remind myself to simply notice it.

I just keep repeating this cycle – I see what comes up, and notice it.

Rob: That sounds productive. I can also see how simply noticing like that is a practice that you can try at all times of the day, in all kinds of places and situations. It doesn't matter if you are still or active – I think I probably do it when riding my bike, or fishing. Or maybe on the train, on the bus, looking out of the window. Maybe in a meeting too, especially if it is a boring one!

It also brings to mind Natalie Wells and Giti Datt's piece on Kundalini yoga in the journal we edited on Conscious Business (Burden and Warwick 2014).

Pete: Yes, and I'd also recommend the work of Dan Siegel (Siegel 2010) which combines an understanding of modern neuroscience with mindfulness. Richard Carson's 'Taming Your Gremlin' (Carson 2003) is also a classic which I have loved for many years.

Of course, many religious traditions also contain similar practices, and these may also be worth exploring. There are countless therapies too – many of which can offer real insights into how we operate.

Rob: What do you think of therapy?

Pete: Personally, I have come to see therapy as a really positive thing. There is still some stigma attached, but I know few people who are truly self-aware, without having done extensive personal self-examination.

And therapy is great for that. Where else do you get the chance to spend an hour a week with another person, someone who has no vested interests other than helping you enquire into who you are and might become?

One approach I would also like to mention is that of Eugene Gendlin (Gendlin, 2010): 'Focusing', and 'Thinking at the Edge', which developed from the former.

What I especially like about Gendlin's ideas is how they start with bodily experience and then connect these to concepts and ideas. This is the other way around from how we often think about life – especially in a world where our dominant paradigm is 'I think therefore I am'.

Focusing puts the body and the emotions at the forefront of our awareness – not just our cognitive processes. We can learn to see emotions as a useful guide, not as a problem.

Along with intuitions, emotions are very useful when dealing with complex situations.

There seem to be many more cognitively-oriented processes out there than bodily-oriented ones. Among the former, I particularly like Kegan and Lahey's (Kegan and Lahey 2009) approach using the 'Four Columns'. This is a really practical approach. You can find out more online, and it was (at least for a while) available as a MOOC[47].

Rob: I think communication practices like Non-Violent Communication (NVC) (Rosenberg 2003), SAVI (Benjamin 2012) and Clear Leadership (Bushe 2010) are also very useful in this way – they encourage us to bring our consciousness to what is happening, to be mindful of what we are saying, as we speak.

---

[47] A massive open online course – at Harvard EDX – http://www.edx.org

They help us become more aware of our needs, our feelings, and of our habits of communication – even our blind spots. They help us make a distinction between what we actually see, or observe, and what we imagine.

But so does even a simple I-statement – in forcing us to state our belief, we become conscious that it is (only) a belief.

There's so much to learn, so much to practise!

Chapter Summary

— Listening is fundamental, but few people do it well.

— Explore the 'core conditions', especially how you can apply them to yourself.

— Writing, and reading our writing, helps us reflect.

— Meditating sounds difficult. But can you 'simply notice'? Over and over again?

— Take your pick: there are body-centred and cognitively-centred practices. Choose one to suit you.

11 Practice – in groups

'Learn some essential practices for working in groups: changing the context, enquiry, and action learning.'

Pete says: But these are mainly individual practices. What about practices that are more fully about the group?

Rob replies: I think we can introduce practices that help groups stop falling into routines so easily. By a group, I mean a management team, a project team, the board of directors and so on.

Sometimes habits and routines are very beneficial and efficient but, as we discussed earlier, there are dangers. There are times when the group needs to start noticing what it is up to.

I find a small change in routine can be really effective in changing the nature of conversation and in helping make new connections between people.

Pete: Can you give some examples?

Rob: Certainly. When holding a meeting, I might try a different location, a different floor, a different building. Or, perhaps, if I am feeling radical, I might suggest an open place like a park. Or not taking notes.

Even slight changes, such as writing board papers in a different style, can make a difference – as we discussed earlier.

But the exact nature of the change isn't the point.

Somehow, changing the setting encourages a different conversation, a conversation that might not otherwise occur in the normal routine. Sometimes it is easy to understand why – for example, in going to a different location people end up talking to different people. Maybe it helps build trust?

Sometimes it isn't so easy to understand why it has an affect.

Pete: Yes, and sometimes the way that people notice is also different, isn't it? For example, if people are required to rely on their memories instead of paper, what they notice (and remember!) changes.

I also encourage people to notice how some of them will resist such initiatives very strongly while others will quickly embrace them.

When I am leading in a group, whether I am the formal leader or not, I try to remember to give voice to whatever I notice. I try to use enquiry as I do this.

So, for example, I might say "I wonder what is happening here?", "How does what is happening in the group affect the results we get?", "How are we responding as an organisation or group?", "How might we do this differently?".

My favourite is probably simply "What's happening?" – which might lead us to ask how what is happening right here, right now, relates to what is happening more broadly, in the organisation.

Rob: Another approach is to invite people into meetings where they would not otherwise be invited. One way to do this is to start with the enquiry "Who needs to be here?".

Typically, this will create the opportunity to bring new people into the conversation, and maybe allow some to leave. In the Open Space movement (Owen 2008), they call the latter the 'Law of Two Feet'. But, personally, I think it should be applicable to every meeting. If you want to leave, then leave!

When new people join a conversation, it may take a very different turn. What new viewpoints do these people bring? What do they notice that everyone else didn't? All that is worth noticing and reflecting on.

Of course, all of this comes with the risk that a meeting held in the local park might seem ridiculous to some. They'll say "Rob, what are you up to? Don't be so silly. Let's just meet where we usually do." My fear might be that my credibility will be undermined. Some groups might love it. But there will always be some who poo-poo this kind of idea.

I think we need to negotiate this risk carefully. But, at the very least, we can use the idea to increase our own awareness of the group we are in. "Why am I so worried, with this particular group, about changing a simple thing, such as the place we meet?"

Pete: Yes, all of this needs to be considered and brought into awareness.

An important discussion is, also, often, what counts as a valuable insight, one from which we might make a decision? For example, some groups only value facts and figures that can be rigorously quantified. When we select information that way, we may miss the wider picture.

Other groups are overly attentive to the big picture – which means the detail may be forgotten.

Drawing attention to what is seen as important can be a difficult discussion. Some people may not like you to question that. There may be individual biases against it.

And, often, we are talking about a group which sits within the context of a wider company or organisation, which shares a similar set of standards for insight and knowledge.

One thing that can be useful, I think, is visits to other organisations – especially those in very different sectors.

When people rub shoulders with other people from different kinds of organisations[48], they may not gain anything immediately obvious.

---

[48] This certainly helped at the MDhub – http://www.mdhub.co.uk – where, by design, MDs from very different industries share insights on the different business models prevalent in each of their industries.

But, at least, it increases awareness of the limitations of a particular approach. Sometimes, they'll then reach out and seek additional perspectives. That is particularly important if we are looking for new and innovative solutions to complex problems.

Rob: What about other ways of talking? Enquiry versus advocacy?

Pete: Yes, and whether there is an internal focus – what is happening inside the business – or an external focus, on the market. Whether conversations are broadly positive or negative?

These are all worth noticing, I think. But, personally, I have always been most excited by the potential of enquiry. Perhaps because I like to ask questions!

To remind us, advocacy means holding a position and trying to persuade others to adopt that point of view. There is so much advocacy in our world – we see it on the media every day. It is sometimes hard to imagine a different way to be within a group.

Enquiry (Schein 2013), in my view, is not so much a way of questioning, although that may be a good way to start. It is also not exactly equivalent to how we normally understand listening – although, again, that is a very good way to start.

I see enquiry as a state of being – it is an openness to what is happening. This is reminiscent of the openness found in many meditative practices. It is a position of 'not knowing', and being receptive and open to whatever emerges – from oneself, from other people, perhaps even from the setting.

Maintaining that state of being is quite difficult, largely because we are so unused to it. Children do it much more naturally than adults, of course. But there are simple ways to encourage people to stay in that state.

One simple method is to talk to another person but only ask questions which are enquiries. It usually takes a bit of coaching to help people start this. It is so easy to respond habitually with an advocacy. But, working in threes, with the third person pointing out advocacies, usually raises awareness.

Of course, it feels really odd to do that. But that is normal when trying something that is outside our usual behavioural repertoire. Noticing that 'oddness' is itself valuable.

Once people are more comfortable with enquiry, they may start to notice all kinds of new things.

Rob: What kind of things?

Pete: Well, as I suggested earlier, we can ask "What is happening in the group?". This may seem a terribly naive question, and elicit blank looks. But, combined with a lengthy pause, something useful and interesting may emerge.

It is, of course, impossible to predict what that may be. It may just be a tendency to want to fill the group with noise. Some people may start speaking. This is very common in groups. It seems some people just can't bear silence.

If that happens, then, that is what is happening!

Rob: We might ask why that happens, but perhaps a more useful question might be to consider what effect this has on the group?

Does it mean, for example, that those who talk a lot in the group dominate what is said and, therefore, what gets agreed or decided? Does it mean that good ideas are not being heard?

Pete: Exactly. Another variant on that is to enquire into how a meeting operates within the broader context of the operation of the business.

Is the pattern one by which, for example, certain people dominate the conversation, and there is then a rush to making decisions and agreeing action?

Then what happens? Who does those actions? Do they get done well? Which ones are left undone, and why? Does this particular organisation value action and busyness over results?

We have all come across organisations where most of the time seems to be spent in meetings. Is this the best way for the group, or the business, to operate? What are the alternatives?

Rob: Those are all great questions. I can see that they may bring a lot to the surface. People may also resist all of that too. I think asking those questions will seem very risky to many people – depending on how much they need to be certain.

Pete: Yes, some people will resist any kind of enquiry, however gentle. But let's think about what happens if we allow an organisation to be dominated by advocacy.

When advocating is favoured, people say things like "Come on Pete, you really need to..." and "Get real – that is just the way it is...".

Ironically, many leaders who rely on their positional power will decry the lack of collaboration, engagement and initiative from employees and other stakeholders. And, then, in their day-to-day behaviour, they themselves, advocate rather than enquire.

I know because I sometimes catch myself doing this too!

If we can't enquire properly, even in a small group like a management team, what chance do we have of learning what our customers or other stakeholders want and need?

How can we develop a meaningful strategy or have any hope of solving difficult problems, unless we can start from a blank sheet – a ***tabla rasa*** – and enquire?

Of course, there is room for advocacy too. But, I think, advocacy often works best when it is a response to an enquiry – not just a bit of habitual, unexamined dogma.

Rob: Enquiry seems to me to also be a central part of action learning. When I use action learning it is usually when an organisation faces really 'wicked problems'[49].

Again, we're talking about the messy and complex. Problems that have no 'right' answer, and are difficult to

---

[49] A problem that is impossible or difficult to resolve because it is contradictory, not complete, or is constantly changing.

understand and even talk about. Problems that we sense may benefit from different perspectives – just to understand what the right questions are.

One way to make progress with wicked problems is also to try some short-term actions, or 'tests', and to explore the results.

I like to work with groups of about 5 to 8 individuals. We work together to seriously consider our own experience. Working in a group, often of peers, is often better than working alone – because of the help, support and challenge that everyone gives each other.

Pete: Yes, I love action learning too. In my experience, people sometimes try to offer each other practical advice or solutions. They try to 'help'. But, often, it is the emotional support, and the challenge to assumptions, that is most valuable.

Rob: Often, the 'helper' gains a lot too – trying to clearly formulate a question or a suggestion can help your own process.

Pete: The point you made earlier about slow thinking is really relevant too. I think it is important to slow the process down. And, personally, I like it when the initial focus is away from action. Many organisations seem to be obsessed by action. They seem to equate activity with results. And believe that, if a meeting doesn't end with action, there is something wrong.

The Eastern principle of *wu wei* (Heider 1997) suggests an alternative. Sometimes, the best action is to do nothing. For example, to let others tire themselves out running around. Waiting for the right moment to move. Busyness can be tiring and exhausting and it clouds our ability to see what is really happening.

We can ask "What is driving this need to move constantly into action?"

Rob: Action does help sometimes, though, doesn't it? In that it gives participants a chance to experiment with the problem?

Pete: Oh yes, it is more a matter of timing for me. All I mean is establishing some simple ground rules, such as guidelines on confidentiality, and how the group will behave if things get sticky. It's just that I notice that sometimes a ground rule on going slowly and avoiding rushing into action or giving solutions helps. It depends on the situation.

Rob: Yes, and what is happening in a specific group. The role of the facilitator initially may be to notice the dynamics in the group, and lightly guide the conversation to ensure people get a fair opportunity to discuss what is on their minds.

I drew Figure 1 to show how the right combination of support and challenge may lead to a more productive experience for participants.

Figure 1

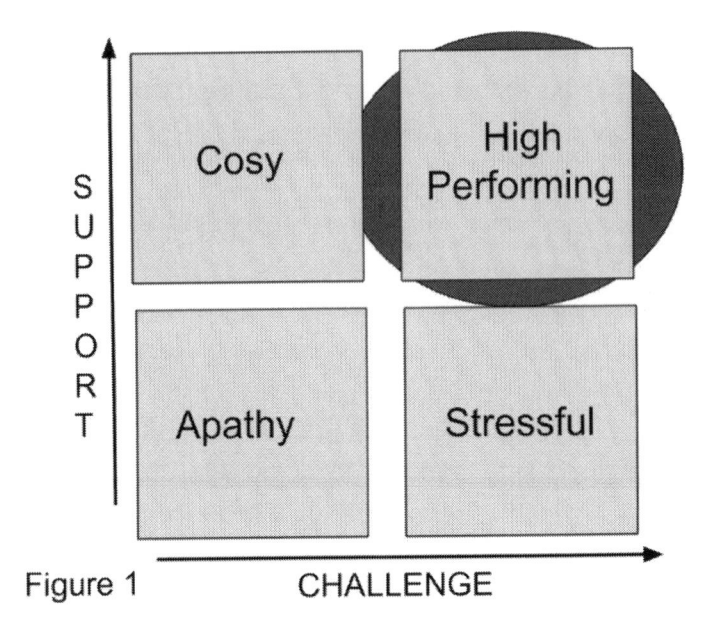

(Y-axis: SUPPORT; X-axis: CHALLENGE)
- Cosy (high support, low challenge)
- High Performing (high support, high challenge)
- Apathy (low support, low challenge)
- Stressful (low support, high challenge)

Once the group is established, it can also facilitate itself to some extent. Once the pattern is set, then they'll typically follow the same pattern, with only a little prodding or reminding every time they meet.

The pattern might include 'checking-in' – people will comment on how they are feeling, and what they are bringing to the group.

Then, one participant starts by describing their 'problem', or issue, to the group. The group discusses the situation with the individual to clarify it. After a few minutes we encourage the individual to restate and clarify the issue.

After that, the group then discusses the problem, focusing on 'coaching' questions that encourage the individual to rethink their problem and come up with a few practical things they could do.

When the group next meets, the actions are often reviewed to see what progress has been made. Or what progress **hasn't been made**. The difficulty of making real progress within a sticky, complex situation often becomes the next issue to discuss.

Pete: Yes, getting stuck in the mud is often a really good place to be!

As you say, part of the facilitator's art is to gracefully hand over control to the participants, and move to a position where only an occasional light touch is needed.

I think there is also a lot of skill involved in selecting the right people and setting up the group at all. The kinds of decisions that are made at the very beginning of the process, such as, who is going to be invited, may have very important consequences (Yalom and Leszc 2008).

Rob: Yes, often action learning sets are only made available to certain kinds of people in an organisation. Middle managers or above.

Perhaps it is best to start with an enquiry: "What will choosing certain people in the organisation mean for the way we achieve our results?", "Should learning sets be available only for senior or middle-ranking staff?", "Who really makes the important decisions?", "Are these really the senior or middle-ranking staff, or is it sometimes the people on the frontline who are making the most important decisions?".

Or "Might mixing people up from different groups, and introducing them to a range of different ideas help?".

Pete: Yes, and other decisions are also important. Things such as whether a group is open or closed to new members, where and how often meetings take place, how and by whom they are facilitated?

These are really important questions for facilitators, sponsors and participants.

Action learning sets are great, but there are so many other techniques. We have only discussed smaller groups, but we could discuss Open Space[50], Appreciative Inquiry[51] and other large group processes too. These are important because they help shift our perspective – for example, to focusing more on our relationships, on the here and now, and on what is going well – rather than looking for problems.

Some colleagues of mine have some online habit-breaking tools which I think show great promise for very large groups – even thousands of people. Just a short programme can help raise awareness of our habits, and help dislodge them[52].

And we haven't really gone into the difficult role of the facilitator. It is easy to imagine facilitation just means getting a group to follow a simple series of steps. But, if the facilitator is not very self-aware themselves, they may bring as many problems as they solve.

---

[50] See the work of Harrison Owen (eg Owen 2008).

[51] See the work of David Cooperrider e.g. http://www.davidcooperrider.com/2012/04/21/positive-organization-development/

[52] Do Something Different – website: http://www.dsd.me

Remember, we are immersed in the complexity – we bring our own 'stuff' with us. I think it is essential that facilitators have done a lot of personal work themselves, so they are aware of at least some of the material they bring with them, and how this might impact on the group.

Creating dependency on the facilitator, coach, or consultant is one problem. Or, if the facilitator does not take enough personal responsibility themselves, and, for example, colludes with a client by supporting them in blaming their team, then they can inadvertently 'license' this approach.

To help with this, individual therapy and personal development is available in many forms, and organisations like the Institute of Group Analysis[53] and the Tavistock Institute[54] provide opportunities to experience the group dynamic, and how you come across in a group.

Rob: Yes, and I have never seen any progress happen overnight. The word 'practice' implies repetition, and that may well be the key to success for all these techniques. Practise may not make perfect, but it certainly helps.

I also think it is a good idea to play around with these techniques – to experiment. Some, such as mindfulness, have been around for millennia. But that doesn't mean we can't modify them, extend them, and find new ways to apply them.

And, of course, we can always invent new processes and techniques.

---

[53] IGA – http://www.groupanalysis.org/

[54] The Tavistock Institute – http://www.tavinstitute.org/

It is a personal journey – as much for the facilitators as for the companies and organisations we work with. Along the way, there are often trials and tribulations. You need to be prepared for resistance – in yourself and in others. But keep experimenting and trying things out. It usually gets better.

Pete: Yes, even resistance can be helpful. If we notice it. Good luck!

Chapter summary

— If in doubt, try changing the physical setting for meetings; this often stirs things up.

— Practise enquiry: ask "what is happening?" or "what is important?"

— Enquiry is a state of being – it is about being open. This is a form of noticing, and a way to lead.

— Action learning is powerful but subtle. Use with care.

— We bring our own 'stuff' as facilitators – so we better be aware of it!

12 Ending... and beginning

'The practices of noticing help. Business can help too. Don't try to seize back control, but don't surrender either. Hope to meet you!'

The story so far

In this book we have talked about the complexity of the world and the challenges of living and working in it. It isn't just complicated, it is 'complex' and chaotic – and that might make it seem hard to understand and live in.

To add to that, we're immersed in it. Our actions, our relationships are all part of the 'mess'.

We talked about the things that make life in businesses and organisations – and indeed in any group – especially difficult. We talked about feelings and emotion, power, and group dynamics. And how ignoring or denying these is only going to add to your problems.

We've considered how the tendency to simplify – '8 step models', checklists or 'organisational frameworks' – can get in the way.

Stories are useful, but we have to be careful not to believe them wholesale. We generate our own, all the time, and it is important to check them out, rather than just assume they are true.

We discussed how noticing the tensions and dynamics in ourselves – being more mindful of them – might be an antidote to some of this. And, if we are brave, how it might help to name these dynamics as they occur. This, for us, is leading.

We discussed purpose – both individual purpose and group purpose – and how, rather than being fixed and handed down from above, it may be more helpful to see purpose as temporary, contextual, relational and 'multi-headed'.

We like Mary Parker Follett's 'Law of the Situation': let what is happening right now, right in front of us, guide our next steps (Follett 2013). Let us take what Follett called our 'orders'– our direction, our aims – from the **situation**, not simply from those with positional power.

Leading mindfully means noticing all of the above.

It means noticing the dominant narrative and metaphors in society, and the stories we make up all the time about each other.

It means noticing and discovering purpose, perhaps even helping it emerge from differences – in opinions, attitudes and points of view.

Having discussed the context, we then focused on what each of us can actually do – the 'practice' of leading more mindfully.

We discussed getting the 'core conditions' right. Going slowly and reflecting. Challenging our 'mind-reading' about others.

How writing can help us reflect. And being mindful – in the sense of sitting, noticing and reflecting.

We talked about what we can do in groups. Changing the setting. Enquiring into what is. Action learning. Going slowly, and resisting 'action'.

And we mentioned the importance of what the facilitator, or leader, brings.

About leading mindfully

When we think of ourselves as leading, we might fall into a fantasy, to start to think of ourselves as a lone hero up against impossible odds. Even so-called 'servant' leadership (Greenleaf 2002), or the 'anti-heroic' style of leadership we described earlier, can be tainted by this attitude.

Can we notice that tendency, that attitude? Can we name it in ourselves? What other attitudes about leading might we have?

For us, leading is a behaviour. It is about what we say and do. But it is also an attitude. An attitude of openness, of enquiry, of curiosity, and of acceptance of self and others.

Leading is about naming the things we see. But the difference between someone who names and hurts, and someone who names and nourishes, is more in their attitude than in the clever words they may utter.

It is from this attitude – from the position we take – that it becomes possible, we believe, to help integration occur. If we are accepting and appreciative of ourselves and others, we may be able to see and understand differences: how we are unique and different, and how everyone else is too.

With this attitude, and from the behaviours of noticing, holding and naming, we may see those differences – those different points of view, those different aims – shift and change.

But our aim is not to achieve some kind of compromise. To quote Mary Parker Follett again (Follett 1918):

> *'Unity, not uniformity, must be our aim. We attain unity only through variety. Differences must be integrated, not annihilated, nor absorbed.'*

Integrating means that new relationships are formed, new connections are made. New perceptions, and more complex, more nuanced understandings. And the whole becomes stronger, and more developed, as a result.

Of course, there is no finality to this. We are talking about 'integrating' – it is a never-ending process. As soon as we think about something, and name it, it becomes static. The process of conversation, of dialogue, by contrast is on-going, and ever-developing.

And be careful. This is easier to say than do. We may think something new – perceive someone differently – but it is only in our on-going actions that we see whether it is a genuine change. All of us can fall back into previous patterns of behaviour.

There is no control, and not much predictability. Instead, to lead is simply to dive into the river – the river of conversation, the river of noticing, the river of integration.

What does it all mean? What can I actually do?

There are problems in the world. Business can be part of the solution. We can all play our part.

But trying just to change the external world probably won't help. Or, at least, we can't predict or control the result.

We can instead focus on changing ourselves. We can become more conscious, more enquiring – especially about our relationships with others.

And we can learn to let go of control, of our desire to get our way. It is only, in any case, by genuinely sharing and integrating our aims with those of others that real shared commitment arises.

With that commitment, we can build groups that have, or tap into, a broader 'collective intelligence'. Groups that work together well, constantly responding to what is front of them. Groups that, together, are able to address issues that individuals simply cannot alone.

And where that collective intelligence continues to grow.

Why bother?

The motivation is there, right in front of us, if we look for it – it's in the 'situation'. We might call it 'purpose', but please don't get distracted by that word. Better to hold purpose lightly, and try to avoid 'fixing' it.

The 'cost'

As the Greeks told us, it is really about **how** we live (Lebell 2013), not **what** we do (or what we achieve). But that is not always easy.

We have touched on some of the difficulty of noticing – and exploring what is going on beneath the surface – in groups and in ourselves.

One way to understand the world is that most of us spend an awful lot of time and energy trying to avoid pulling up the carpet and taking a look at what is there.

Is that why we are all so busy? Why social media is such a success? Do we seek distraction?

Is that why business 'builds' so much? Is avoidance the source of the creative destruction that Schumpeter[55] described in our broad economic process – of which business is such an important part. Is this behind our obsession with economic growth?

And what **is** under the carpet? We think, underlying pretty much everything – the difficulty of seeing more of reality, of noticing, of enquiry, the difficulty of speaking up, the difficulty of feeling things – is fear.

Some of this fear is real. Some less so. Other people **can** impact our lives – negatively as well as positively. There is also always an existential fear lurking somewhere. But some fear is neurotic, and really not very helpful.

---

[55] Joseph Schumpeter see e.g. https://en.wikipedia.org/wiki/Joseph_Schumpeter.

There is probably no sense in trying to eradicate fear. Instead, we believe we can 'work' with fear and anxiety. To incorporate it more usefully into our working and personal lives.

We believe that noticing, awareness, and enquiry – being more mindful – at least give the possibility of accepting, and even integrating, that fear.

It's our journey too

As we said up front, we're not pretending to be masters of this. We're learning as we go. Experimenting and trying things out. Alongside many colleagues.

These ideas may seem strange to you. They may even feel threatening. Perhaps that is worth an enquiry?

We notice these ideas arise, again and again, and we hope it has been helpful for you to read them – just as it has helped us to write them down.

We are happy to engage further. Please use the references and notes to find communities[56] of people interested in exploring such ideas further. Or get in touch via the contact details at the end of the book.

We hope to meet you.

Chapter summary

— Leading means holding, and noticing, differences, and helping others notice differences too.

---

[56] E.g. Conscious Business UK on LinkedIn.

— Leading means integrating – in ourselves, and in groups. Integrating opinions, attitudes, points of view, aims and desires.

— Integrating means bringing forth new relationships – seeing the world in new ways, and seeing each other in new ways too.

— There's a great opportunity out there – to be part of the solution. But don't forget – try to stay awake, especially to what *you* are doing!

— There's little to fear but fear itself[57] – but even a little fear can harm us if we don't recognise it, and speak up about it. So can we integrate that anxiety too?

— You're not alone. Maybe we'll meet along the way?

---

[57] Roosevelt first inauguration speech, 4th March 1933.

References

Ackoff R (1979) The Future of Operational Research is Past. *The Journal of the Operational Research Society*, 30(2), 93–104.

Beck R (2014) Conformity – Elevator Candid Camera. *Vimeo*, Available from: https://vimeo.com/61349466 (accessed 3 March 2015).

Beer S (2009) *Think Before You Think: Social Complexity and Knowledge of Knowing*. Oxford: Wavestone Press.

Benjamin, B, Yeager, A, and Simon, A. (2012) *Conversation Transformation*. New York: McGraw Hill.

Berne E (2010) *Games People Play: The Psychology of Human Relationships*. New York: Penguin.

Bolton R (2011) *People Skills: How to Assert Yourself, Listen to Others and Resolve Conflicts*. New Haven and London: Simon and Schuster.

Boroson M (2007) *The One Moment Master: Stillness for People on the Go*. Random House.

Bourdieu P (1990) *The Logic of Practice*. Cambridge, UK: Polity Press.

Bourdieu P (1998) Is a Disinterested Act Possible? In: Bourdieu P (ed.), *Practical Reason: On the Theory of Action*, Cambridge, UK: Polity Press.

Bowlby E (2008) *Attachment: Volume One of the Attachment and Loss Trilogy*. Random House.

Burden P and Warwick R (2014) The Purpose and Practice of Conscious Business – Editorial. *e-Organisations and*

People, Journal of the Association of Management Education and Development, 21(1), 3–9.

Bushe G (2010) *Clear Leadership: Sustaining Real Collaboration and Partnership at Work.* Boston: Nicholas Brealey.

Carson R (2003) *Taming Your Gremlin.* New York: Harper Collins.

Chaplin C (1936) *Modern Times.*

Dalal F (1998) *Taking the Group Seriously – Towards a Post-Foulkesian Group Analytic Theory.* London and Philadelphia: Jessica Kingsley Publishers.

De Mello A (1990) *Awareness.* Michigan: Zondervan.

Dewey J (2007) *Democracy and Education.* Teddington: Echo Library.

Elias N (1978) *What is Sociology?* New York: Columbia University Press.

Flyvbjerg B (1998) *Rationality and Power – Democracy in Practice.* Chicago: Chicago University.

Flyvbjerg B (2001) *Making social science matter: Why social inquiry fails and how it can succeed again.* Cambridge, UK: Cambridge University Press.

Follett M (1918) *The New State: Group Organization, the Solution of Popular Government.* Literary Licensing LLC.

Follett M (2013) *Freedom & co-ordination: Lectures in business organization.* Oxford: Routledge.

Follett M (2014) *The Essential Mary Parker Follett: Ideas We Need Today.* Héon F, Davis A, Jones-Patulli J, et al. (eds), F. Heon, A. Davis, S. Damart, J. Jones-Patulli.

Foulkes S (1983) *Introduction to Group Analytic Psychotherapy.* Karnac Books.

Gendlin E (2010) *Focusing.* Random House.

Gergen K (2009) *Relational being: Beyond self and community.* Oxford: Oxford University Press.

Goleman D (2009) *Working with Emotional Intelligence.* London: Bloomsbury.

Greenleaf R (2002) *Servant leadership: A journey into the nature of legitimate power and greatness.* Paulist Press.

Griffin D, Shaw P and Stacey R (1998) Speaking of complexity in management theory and practice. *Organization*, 5(3).

Haidt J (2006) *The Happiness Hypothesis: Finding Modern Truth in Ancient Wisdom.* Basic Books.

Heider J (1997) *The Tao of Leadership: Lao Tzu's Tao Te Ching Adapted for a New Age.* Atlanta: Humanics New Age.

Héon F, Jones-Patulli J, Damart S, et al. (eds) (2014) *Mary Parker Follett: Ideas We Need Today.*

Juul J (1995) *Your Competent Child: Toward A New Paradigm in Parenting and Education.* Bloomington: Baloa Press.

Kegan R and Lahey L (2009) *Immunity to Change.* Boston: Harvard Business Review Press.

Kofman F (2006) *Conscious Business – How to Build Value Through Values.* Boulder: Sounds True.

Korzybski A (1931) A Non-Aristotelian System and its Necessity for Rigour in Mathematics and Physics. In: *American Mathematical Society at the New Orleans, Louisiana, meeting of the American Association for the Advancement of Science, Reprinted in Science and Sanity, 1933*, pp. 747–61.

Lakoff G and Johnson M (2003) *Metaphors We Live By.* Chicago: Chicago University.

Laloux F (2014) *Reinventing Organizations: A Guide to Creating Organizations Inspired by the Next Stage of Human Consciousness.* Nelson Parker.

Lebell S (2013) *The Art of Living: The Classical Manual on Virtue, Happiness, and Effectiveness.* Harper Collins.

Machiavelli N (1984) *The Prince.* Oxford Wor. Bondanella P (ed.), Oxford: Oxford University Press.

Mackey J and Sisodia R (2014) *Conscious Capitalism – Liberating the Heroic Spirit of Business.* Boston: Harvard Business Review Press.

McGilchrist I (2009) *The Master and His Emissary: The Divided Brain and the Making of the Western World.* Yale: Yale University Press.

Mead G H (1934) *Mind, Self, & Society.* Chicago: Chicago University.

Menzies-Lyth I (1959) 'Selected Essays: Containing Anxiety in Institutions, Vol. 1.'

Mindtools (2015) The Ladder of Inference Avoiding 'Jumping to Conclusions'. Available from: http://www.mindtools.com/pages/article/newTMC_91.htm (accessed 18 March 2015).

Mindell, A. (1992) *The Leader as Martial Artist: An Introduction to Deep Democracy* (1st ed.). San Francisco: Harper.

Morgan G (2006) *Images of Organization.* London: Sage.

Oshry B (1999) *Leading Systems: Lessons from the Power Lab.* San Francisco: Berrett Koehler Inc.

Owen H (2008) *Open Space Technology: A User's Guide.* San Francisco: Berrett Koehler Inc.

Rock D (2009) *Your Brain at Work.* New York: Harper Collins.

Rogers C (1967) *A Therapist's View of Psychotherapy: On Becoming a Person.* Constable and Company.

Rodgers C (2007) *Informal Coalitions: Mastering the Hidden Dynamics of Organizational Change.* Basingstoke: Palgrave Macmillan.

Rosenberg M (2003) *Nonviolent Communication: A Language of Life.* 2nd ed. Encinitas: Puddle Dancer Press.

Schein E (2003) *DEC is dead, long live DEC.* San Francisco: Berrett Koehler Inc.

Schein E (2013) *Humble Inquiry: The Gentle Art of Asking Instead of Telling.* San Francisco: Berrett Koehler Inc.

Seligman F (2002) *Authentic Happiness.* New York: Free Press.

Siegel D (2010) Mindsight: change your brain and your life. Scribe Publications.

Tate W (2012) *Centre For Progressive Leadership – A White Paper Managing leadership from a systemic perspective.* London, Available from:

http://www.londonmet.ac.uk/media/london-metropolitan-university/london-met-documents/faculties/guildhall-faculty-of-business-and-law/london-metropolitan-business-school/research-centres/cpl/publications/CPL-WP---Managing-leadership-from-a-systemic-perspective---(William-Tate).pdf (accessed 18 March 2015).

The Department of Health (2001) The report of the public inquiry into children's heart surgery at the Bristol Royal Infirmary 1984-1995: learning from Bristol. Available from: http://webarchive.nationalarchives.gov.uk/+/www.dh.gov.uk/en/Publicationsandstatistics/Publications/PublicationsPolicyAndGuidance/DH_4005620(accessed 18 March 2015).

Torbert W (2004) *Action Inquiry: The Secret of Timely and Transforming Leadership.* Berrett-Koehler Publishers.

Warwick R and Burden P (2013) Exploring Conscious Business Practice – Editorial. *e-Organisations and People, Journal of the Association of Management Education and Development*, 20(4), 3–9.

Weick K (1995) *Sensemaking in Organizations.* Thousand Oaks: Sage.

Whittle S and Izod K (eds) (2009) *Mind-ful Consulting.* London: Karnac.

Yalom I and Leszc M (2008) *The Theory and Practice of Group Psychotherapy.* 5th ed. Basic Books.

About the authors

Pete Burden @peteburden
http://www.linkedin.com/in/peteburden

Pete helps purposeful people bring new business ideas to life. He acts as a coach and a sounding board, helping teams develop their ability to work together, and to deliver business projects. He works to improve communication, bringing a focus on 'enquiry' in the face of complexity.

He has worked on a huge variety of purposeful ventures and projects over nearly three decades – with more than 50 management teams and MDs. He has held several Director-level roles, and has been involved in several purposeful start-ups.

In the last few years he has been helping challenge the dominant discourse about business, leadership and management, by exploring and writing about the idea of 'Conscious Business'.

Until 2012 he was Exec Chair of a social media business that explored the future of work. In the early noughties he helped create a brand new way to deliver business support to SME MDs – through peer-to-peer learning.

In the '90s he helped the BBC and Which? find new ways to cope with the emerging digital world. Prior to all that he worked for a large but very entrepreneurial company (DEC), now part of HP.

Rob Warwick @smilerob
http://uk.linkedin.com/pub/rob-warwick/2/43/b01/

Rob has a doctorate in healthcare policy, focusing on the interaction between policy and frontline practice. This was gained whilst working as Head of Strategic Change for a large NHS organization where he worked closely with the English Department of Health on a national healthcare initiative.

In addition to 14 years in a variety of NHS management positions, Rob has 8 years' experience in consultancy.

Rob has held academic roles with Cass Business School and London Metropolitan University and is currently with the University of Chichester; subjects include healthcare, strategy, management and leadership.

Rob's particular area of interest is the role of narrative in organisations and personal development and how this might be used to explore reflexivity, complexity and power relations in groups.

Connected with this, Rob is also engaged in 'Conscious Business' where people in organisations think beyond profit and towards human development and growth, wider stakeholder needs, both now and for the future.

Printed in Great Britain
by Amazon.co.uk, Ltd.,
Marston Gate.